Just Left Of Center

Just Left
Of Center

*These Are True Stories,
You Can't Make This Stuff Up*

Just Left Of Center
*These Are True Stories,
You Can't Make This Stuff Up*

© 2015 Fran Gruen

All Rights Reserved. The author grants no assignable permission to reproduce for resale or redistribution. This license is limited to the individual purchaser and does not extend to others. Permission to reproduce these materials for any other purpose must be obtained in writing from the publisher except for the use of brief quotations within book chapters.

Disclaimer
All rights reserved. No part of this book may be used or reproduced by any means, graphic, scanning, electronic, or mechanical, including photocopying, recording, taping or by any information storage retrieval system without the written permission of the publisher except in the case of brief quotations embodied in critical articles and reviews.

ISBN-10:   1942731124
ISBN-13:   978-1-942731-12-2

        Published by M&B Global Solutions Inc.
            United States of America (USA)

Just Left Of Center

*These Are True Stories,
You Can't Make This Stuff Up*

Fran Gruen

Just Left Of Center

Dedication

To my siblings, Ed and Theresa –
Ed, I finally know the true story of who broke the lamp shade:
You threw it correctly, I could have caught your throw,
But baby sister Theresa reached up and deflected the pillow,
Thus, Theresa is the one who broke the lamp shade.

Just Left Of Center

Contents

Preface 9

I Chase Buses, Don't I 11

She Flies Through The Air
With the Greatest of Ease 19

What They Don't Tell You
About Having a Heart Cath 35

Yoga Is a Four-Letter Word 49

You've Got To Be Kidding,
My Body Is Not Made That Way 63

How I Spent My Summer Vacation 77

An Open Door Is Not Always a Good Thing 115

And In Conclusion 124

Acknowledgements 126

About the Author 128

Just Left Of Center

Preface

Picture this scenario: someone asks you and me what we did today, and it happens we both went grocery shopping. You would answer, "I went grocery shopping." I would answer, "I opened my refrigerator and heard an echo. I knew I couldn't put it off any longer, so I got in my car and headed for that much-disorganized building called a grocery store. After cruising the parking lot for five minutes, I parked and went in to grab a cart and then the weekly sale flyer. Now, can anyone tell me why they put the sale flyer just inside the door where there is always at least one traffic jam? They should put a nice little reading room there off to the side."

That is the way my mind works most of the time, *Just Left of Center*.

This is a collection of true stories that have happened in my crazy ride through life. I'm sure a therapist would have a deep, babbling explanation for my constant use of humor. But the truth is I like to make people laugh. Life is too serious. Smile or I'll tell you a story. Humor has gotten me this far and I intend to take as many of you with me as I can. I hope to capture your funny bone with my stories just as great storytellers such as columnist Erma Bombeck and stand-up comedian Bob Newhart captured mine.

In high school, I was on the forensics team and we would travel by school bus to other competing schools. A few of us would sit in the back and listen to a classmate recite the monologues of our favorite comedians at the time. If we got to the school before he finished a monologue, we waited to get off the bus until he finished the story.

I don't expect my short stories to instill such loyalty. But could you pretend they do if we should ever meet? Thanks!

I Chase Buses, Don't I

This true story ties in my love of gardening. I tell it to all the bus tour groups that I guide through our local botanical garden. I usually tell it to the folks while on the bus saying goodbye. The setting obviously makes the story that much more amusing. So here is what happened the day I had to chase a bus.

A few years ago, our botanical garden in Green Bay, Wisconsin, offered a bus trip down to the Chicago Flower Show. This show is held in the spring at the Navy Pier convention center with millions of flowers. In this case, I didn't have to drive to Chicago, which was a big plus. I had talked about it with friends at home and at work without any takers. So I would have to travel alone, but I would see lots of flowers.

I went to bed the night before after setting my alarm for 5:30 a.m. The bus was to leave the garden promptly at 7:00 a.m. I fell asleep with visions of hydrangeas dancing in my head. I woke to the radio alarm and got ready for a fun day of flowers and more flowers. I was all ready and saw I had plenty of time. It takes less than ten minutes to get to the garden and the bus was to leave the garden promptly at 7:30 a.m. At least, that's the time I had in my head.

I left that morning to go to the botanical garden with those same visions from last night. As I approached the last intersection before the botanical garden, I noticed a tour bus at the same intersection heading in the direction I had just come from. I remember thinking, "Gee, there's another tour bus; I wonder where they are going?" I pulled into the botanical garden parking lot and the first thing I noticed was that although there were plenty of cars in the lot, no one was standing around. I began to have a sinking feeling. I calmly reached for a copy of the trip itinerary and saw what I did not want to see. That's right, the bus was to leave the garden promptly at 7:00 a.m. and I had missed the bus.

I continued reading and saw that the bus would also stop at a hotel in Manitowoc, less than an hour away. Now it was decision time. Should I just go home and pout all day, or should I chase the bus and get on for the rest of the ride to Chicago? It's a little late to mention this, but I love flowers, I love to see what new and exciting varieties are out and how they will grow in my yard. I just plain love flowers. So, with this disclaimer, you know what I did. That's right, I chased the bus.

This immediately brought up a dilemma for me: if the route took the bus from Green Bay to Manitowoc, the bus would be going over the Tower Drive Bridge, which is as high as it sounds. As much as I love flowers, that's how much I hate bridges. Not all bridges, just the ones I have had to cross. Despite my fears, I headed for the Tower Drive Bridge and drove over it. Not only did I drive over it, I drove very fast over it. Miracle of miracles, I made it alive.

With renewed confidence, I continued on to Manitowoc. I got to the hotel where the bus was stopping to pick up more passengers. As I took the exit to the hotel, I could see the bus. Unfortunately, what I saw was the back of the bus leaving one driveway while I entered another driveway. Oh, the sheer irony of it all. So close and yet so far. This just isn't my day. I decided that since I had the whole day off, I might as well continue following the bus for now. I banked on the chance that it would make a stop for the passengers to stretch their legs before hitting Milwaukee another hour down the interstate.

As the miles rolled by, I began to reassess my decision. Maybe it was not such a great idea after all. I was close to Milwaukee and I really did not want to drive through it, so I made an executive decision. I decided to turn around and go home. So I pulled off the highway at Port Washington and pulled into the parking lot of one of the many fast food chain restaurants. After finishing a breakfast sandwich in the restaurant, I decided to use the rest room before I headed for home.

I was going in the door as another woman was coming out. My people recognition radar was working just fine, which is why I said, "Sue, what are you doing here?" Sue replied, "Fran, what are you doing here? I thought you were going to Chicago". Sue is one of the co-workers to whom I had mentioned the flower show. We got out of the way of foot traffic and discussed our plans for the day. It seems that Sue was headed to the Chicago Flower Show with her husband and daughter in their own vehicle so they could do other shopping while in Chicago. I told Sue my tale of woe. Then this great big light bulb came on above my head and I asked a brilliant question, one that would change the course of my day. "Sue, could I ask you a really big favor? Would you let me travel with you to the Chicago Flower Show?"

Of course Sue said yes, for two reasons. First of all, Sue is a kind and caring person; and second of all, she was probably a little nervous about the crazed look in my eyes and decided to keep me calm. She introduced me to her family, and we got into their car and headed for our destination.

There was a sad experience shortly after we left Port Washington; we lost a member of the passenger list. As we were on the entry ramp to the interstate, Sue asked her daughter Kathy, sitting in the back seat with me, to please pass her the breakfast sandwich she had ordered to go. Kathy got a funny look on her face and told her mother that when she got in the car she had put the bag of food on top of the car! Hearing this, Sue's husband carefully pulled over on the ramp, their soon-to-be ex-daughter got out and checked the roof. Nothing, nada, zip. She meekly got back in the car and we proceeded down the ramp on the way to Chicago. There was a short discussion about the loss of our fellow passenger. The rest of the trip was very quiet.

We arrived at the Navy Pier, home of the Chicago Flower Show. I thanked my newly found friends for the ride and headed for the millions of flowers. I went to the admission booth to buy a ticket. I didn't even entertain the possibility of mentioning that somewhere in the bowels of the convention center was a person who did have my ticket. But I was favoring the path of least resistance. I explained to the ticket attendant about what had happened that day. I asked her if they had a break room set up for the bus drivers and tour guides. She told me where I could find the bus drivers, and I headed for it before enjoying the flower show.

It was difficult; I felt someone or something tugging at my arm to go in those magic doors leading to the flower show. I checked out the drivers' room and actually found the one who had driven "our" bus from Green Bay. I started to tell him my story, but he interrupted with, "So you're the one, but how did you get here?" I then quietly and slowly finished my story. I ended with a request to get on the bus at the end of the show and get dropped off at the restaurant in Port Washington where I had left my car. He agreed and then told me when and where he would be picking up. I intended to be there at least fifteen minutes early.

And now, the moment you've all been waiting for … I stepped into the Chicago Flower Show. It was worth the wait, worth the convoluted route taken to get here. It was truly the largest convention hall I had ever seen this side of the Mississippi. There were vases of flowers, garden beds full of flowers, flowers adorning dining tables, and flowers for sale. I was in flower nirvana! I had, of course, lost a little time getting to this point, so I proceeded to move double time through the exhibits.

My progress was hampered by having to stop and talk with: the botanical garden bus tour guide; at least three different people from the tour bus that I knew; and my dear friend Sue and her family. I informed the first what had happened and my request of riding back with them to my car; the second group I had to tell my story of chasing the bus; and the last group I informed that I no longer needed their transport services. But believe me; I was at the appointed loading zone with fifteen minutes to spare.

The bus pulled up, and I and my new fellow passengers got on. I had to wait until everyone was seated to see where the empty seat was, during which time I told my chasing the bus story more than two times. The end of the day went much more smoothly than the beginning. When we got to Port Washington, the bus driver pulled off the highway and into the restaurant parking lot where I had left my car. I got off with many farewells and a great big Thank You to the tour guide and bus driver. I got settled in my car, and followed the bus back to Green Bay.

Just Left Of Center

She Flies Through The Air With The Greatest Of Ease

There I was, minding my own business, when a trusted friend (I am re-evaluating that description) asked me what I was doing the next Sunday. I replied with, "Nothing."

Error in judgment No. 1.

This then-trusted friend, Jan, asked me if I would like to go along with her on a road rally in the Green Bay area sponsored by her church. I fell for it, hook, line and mileage. I said it sounded like fun and would join her on Sunday.

Error in judgment No. 2.

I was then given the details of when and where, followed closely by the whom. Oh, by the way, Paula also is on our team. Jan thought it would be a friendly gesture to include me with her. There also was a last-minute cancellation of one of the participants.

So there we were, Sunday morning, the number three car to leave the church parking lot.

The Starting Line

Let's set the scene: Jan is driving her car, Paula is in the front passenger seat, dubbed the jump-out-of-the-car-and-look-for-the-clue seat. I'm in the back, hoping to fall asleep as I usually do. We were handed the directions by the author, Dave, also known as the sadist. As Jan pulls out of the parking lot, Paula starts reading the directions. They are *three pages long*.

I sigh and try to get comfortable, sinking down in my seat so the team members in front will forget I'm there. The first clue has to do with a tank and turning right, but they didn't look for the tank and proceeded to turn left at the first intersection. I spoke up – error in judgment No. 3 – and suggested we turn around and go in the other direction. After all, the other direction is the direction car number two went when they left the parking lot, and car number two was occupied by the parents of Dave the sadist.

I understand it took quite a while for them to talk to him after the road-rally debacle. As we found out later, neither of us made the right – that is, correct – turn. We were supposed to go straight at that intersection to Abrams Street. (Did you know there is a connection between the word "Tank" and the name "Abrams?")

Exactly. Nobody knew except Dave the sadist.

Off We Go

Paula reads the next clue and we discuss it (yes, I've joined in by now), offering our own interpretations and naturally finding they are all different. Since Jan can't really stop in traffic, she drives on blindly while we carry on a more detailed discussion of what the clue means.

By the time we get to the "Fireman's Friend" clue, Paula has read the directions up and back. Before I could stop myself, I took them into my own possession.

Error in judgment No. 4.

At that point, we had nearly reached our friend Melanie's house on Finger Road. I convinced Jan to turn around and go back into town in an attempt at reorientation.

We then found ourselves by the car dealers "hidden behind a mall," which is their slogan to help customers find them behind Green Bay's East Town Mall. We are to look for the "VIN of the Z car." First of all, I don't know how I know what a VIN is, but lucky for us, I do. VIN stands for the vehicle identification number of a car, mounted on the dashboard near the windshield. Therefore, I know we are looking for a car, with a Z on it and it's blue. (By the way, I'm not showing off about the VIN. I just figured someone reading this tale may not know and will spend many sleepless nights trying to figure it out.)

So there we are, cruising (unless you're Dave the sadist, who can't spell, and he would be "crusing") up and down the street, looking for a "Z car." We all suddenly felt the need to raise our voices at that point. It got quite noisy in that car.

As we are about to pull into one of the car lots, we see a familiar car approaching. It is the second car out of the slots, Joyce and Mike, the parents of Dave the sadist. Now you have to understand this sub-competition of the competition, as it will come into play later in the story. Jan has one goal for this road rally: beat Mike. Mike's one goal is to beat everyone. So Jan was thrilled to see we were ahead at this point.

And then, there it was: the Z car. Paula jumps out of the car and races for the clue while Jan plays lookout, hoping Mike hasn't spotted us spotting the clue.

Needless to say, we saw much more of the east side of Green Bay in the next hour or two. I understand that if we were to have finished, we would have been to the west side and ended in Ashwaubenon, a suburb on the city's southwest side. The fatal directions were read by me, I must admit, before we had even reached page two. We were in the Baird's Creek area on the far-east side, and were supposed to find out who had gotten the most recent hole-in-one on hole number eleven.

The Fateful Eleventh Hole

Who had made the most recent hole-in-one on hole number eleven? That was our current mission, and frankly, Scarlett, I didn't give a flying Frisbee what the answer really was.

You see, the air conditioner in Jan's car had not been working correctly, and I was hot. Not just hot, but sweating, hair-wet, hard-to-breathe hot. It was at this point that there, on our left, we saw it – a golf course. And not just any golf course. Oh no – this one happened to be a disk golf course. That's right, Frisbee golf, just like a young friend, also named Dave, used to tell me about.

So we drive up to the parking lot, and as Jan's car climbs the slope, I realize the course is set up on some major hills and valleys. This must be a real big challenge for the golfers. We pulled into the parking lot and looked around at the other cars. There are no cars from our group of road-rally fools – excuse me – road rally players. Jan is openly happy, though. She is again ahead of Mike. I hand Paula the directions and a pen, and she does what she is assigned to do: jump out of the car and look for the clue.

Paula walks up to a small building that looks like the starting point for the course and disappears around the side. This is the last we see of her for fifteen minutes or so. Two more cars show up from our group in the meantime, one of them being Joyce and Mike's. I decided it was high time for a cat nap and quickly made it so, only to be rudely awakened a few minutes later by Jan saying, "Where is she? She's been gone a long time!"

This completely chased away my vision of all the weeds I could have pulled from my flower beds. We had seen Mike go around the same building and not come back, so we both got out of the car and started heading toward the Bermuda Triangle building. They were nowhere to be found. Could they have been abducted by aliens? Would we have to call in Mulder and Scully?

Jan headed to the left and I walked through the pavilion. Still no Paula in sight. I was growing frustrated, and left my post to head back to Jan. Jan said she had spotted both Paula and Mike down a particular hill, obviously headed for the eleventh hole. I wandered over to the other side of the pavilion and saw the pair.

Paula and Mike were walking up the hill on the far side of the pavilion. As they got closer, I noticed Paula was walking with her arms away from her body, like someone would when all wet. I judged she had fallen in a creek. By the looks of it, she was covered in mud and dirt.

Error in judgment No. 5.

As they got closer, I noticed a few things which made me reconsider the situation. It was certainly *not* mud on her face, but blood! Paula had a mess of blood all the way down the center of her face, and it was still pouring from somewhere. She was walking in that funny way because she couldn't see where she was going, gingerly holding her broken glasses in her hand.

The poor woman was puffing pretty hard by the time she got to us, but we had to ask the obvious question: Who got the hole in one on eleven? No, no, we weren't that crass! We immediately asked what happened. Paula relayed she had fallen down the hill and landed on her face. Some golfers had told her to take a short cut down this one hill to get to the eleventh hole faster. What they didn't tell her was she had to be part mountain goat to successfully do it.

Footnote: I know this is not where a footnote belongs, and actually this is probably not really a footnote. But to further set the scene, Mike told Jan the next day about Paula's flight. You see, Paula didn't just fall down the hill. Paula was going down the hill, she slipped and was airborne, and Mike wasn't sure exactly how long her flight lasted. She was airborne, landed flat on her face, and then slid farther down the hill, in her face-first position. Where's the video camera when you need it? I think we could have discovered a new theory on aeronautics.

Jan went to find a towel in her car while I took Paula into the pavilion's restroom. Mike came in to see how she was and then left. This is where that sub-competition comes into play. Jan arrived with the towel, and we proceeded to clean up the walking wounded. We got her cleaned up as best as we could, although her nose was still bleeding a little. Summary of the damages: she had a bruise on her elbow; her nose, forehead and chin were scraped; she had bitten her lower lip; and her nose was still bleeding.

We left the pavilion, eventually making our way back to the car. All the other participants had come and gone while we were tending to Paula's wounds.

Where Does It Hurt?

Once we were settled back in Jan's car, we discussed what to do and in what order. Paula had, by this time, said, "I'm sorry for ruining your day," at least eight times; to the point where I advised her if she said it one more time, I was going to slap her upside the head. But before Jan started the car, she asked Paula a question, a question fitting of a trial lawyer. It was also a question she knew the answer to: "I suppose you don't feel like finishing the road rally now. What do you want to do?"

Paula obviously was going to say she did not feel like finishing the rally. She needed to go back to her car in the church parking lot so she could get her spare pair of glasses, as she really was blind without them.

We headed down the hilly driveway; and may I point out that we drove, we did not fly. Paula had already done that. Again, she opened her mouth and said she was sorry for ruining our day. True to my word, I slapped her upside the head.

In my defense, I did it gently. After all, I know enough about first aid to remember if a person has a possible concussion and/or broken nose, you should be careful with them. But come on, I warned her. It's not my fault she didn't believe my promise.

We drove back to the church parking lot. There I said hello to my car, Paula got her spare pair of glasses, and we piled back into Jan's car. I would just like to make one comment here about those spare glasses. I hate to keep you in suspense, waiting, but you know I can't pass this up without a comment. How many people do you know who carry a spare pair of glasses in their car? Including Paula, I know one.

Again, Jan asked Paula what she wanted to do. Paula's answer was, "I think I should maybe get checked out at St. V's (St. Vincent Hospital). I'm sorry for ruining your day."

And yes, once again, I slapped her. She really is a slow learner. Either that or she had amnesia from a concussion. Off we went to St. V's, where Jan let us off at the doors while she went to park. We waited for her before proceeding to the Emergency Room reception desk. Paula gave the ward clerk the basic outline of her medical complaint. It took me a while to figure out why the clerk looked at Paula with such a skeptical look. We had done a darn good job of cleaning up Paula, and apparently she was finding it hard to believe the story. She gave us a form to fill out and we all sat in the waiting area.

The chairs were very comfortable, with backs that had a little give to them. Visions of a much-anticipated nap popped into my head. The triage nurse came and got Paula, so Jan and I settled in. We were just discussing that it was well past 3 p.m. and we hadn't eaten since breakfast. Not a good thing for my medical condition. As we were about to decide where to get a snack, the triage nurse came out of her office and called our names. We looked at each other and got up apprehensively.

(By the way, how about all them big words? Just showing off my college education.)

So again, I put my naptime on hold and we went to see what the nurse wanted. She told us she was ready to take Paula back to an exam room and we should come along. My mind was screaming, "NO, I want my nap, I want my nap, I want my nap!" I didn't get it. Like good people, we followed the nurse back to the exam room.

Error in judgment No. 6.

There we were, Paula in the general-issue hospital gown, Jan on the courtesy phone to let Dave the sadist know there is nowhere he can hide from us, and me, trying to get comfortable in the chair allotted to me. I was trying to look concerned, not just tired and hungry.

We then proceeded to the twenty-minute ER visit. For those of you who have never been to an ER, I do not mean that we were in and out of there in twenty minutes. Oh contraire, mon ami, (I believe that's French for "big dummy.") That means that we waited twenty minutes between each visit from a different emergency-room team player, a sort of twenty-minute tag team. I think they had a timer outside the exam room they kept resetting every time one of the team players left. Team members number one and two came in. They were from registration, with number two being in training. They asked a few questions, and number one showed number two how to work the computer.

The twenty minutes pass. Team member number three comes in, the nurse in charge of Paula's care. She asks a few questions and hands Paula a gown, only to find something wrong with it (the gown, not Paula). She leaves to get a different one. Another twenty minutes pass. Team member number four arrives, another nurse who wants to know why Paula doesn't have the gown on yet and makes her put on the original one. She asks a few more questions. Jan asks about making a call and is told to use the phone on the wall; that's what it's there for. Number four leaves to find the doctor. The next twenty-minute interval slides by.

Finally, team member number five comes in, the doctor. Now we're getting somewhere! More questions and an exam ensue, and he says he would like to get an X-ray of her nose. He leaves. Twenty minutes pass. In walks team member number six, the X-ray technician. She takes Paula away, and Jan and I are peacefully alone for – that's right – twenty minutes. They finally come back, and we wait for another twenty minutes. Team member five pokes his head in, but makes sure he does not actually step into the room. He tells Paula her nose is not broken, so he's sending her home with pain medication. Still another twenty minutes later, team member four returns, and leaves because ...

Sidebar - The Phone Call To Dad

Paula was now on the patient courtesy phone used earlier by Jan. She wanted to call her dad to see how he was doing. She didn't want to use the courtesy phone because her Dad had caller ID and she didn't want him to worry. Someone in the room, (her name begins with J) told Paula caller ID would not work because of HIPAA privacy laws. But, as Paula was about to learn, not everyone updates their protocols.

First, we hear Paula asking her Dad how he is and did he take a nap, then she's saying something about how she took a little tumble down a hill and she wanted to get checked out. Jan and I look at each other with the same look on our faces – oops!

E. R. Continued

Twenty minutes later, the nurse returns and gives Paula her written discharge orders and a vial of pills: Vicodin. We finally were set free of that little room and head for daylight. Jan goes straight for her car and I walk slowly to the door with Paula. We got in and head back to the church parking lot.

Unfortunately, Paula is a slow learner, and she spoke those fateful words: "I'm sorry for ruining your day."

Yes, for the third time that day, I slapped her upside the head. After all, now we knew for certain she did not have a concussion or a broken nose!

Home, Jan

We got back to the church parking lot, battered and torn (well, at least Paula was battered and torn). Jan asked Paula if she thought she could get home on her own. I asked Paula if she wanted me to drive her.

Error in judgment No. 7.

The answer, of course, was, "Yes, maybe that would be better."

I got into the driver's seat of Paula's Saturn, not without some gymnastics. Her steering wheel was set quite low and I had to make myself horizontal to get in under it. Since Jan had never been to Paula's apartment, I kept checking in the rearview mirror to make sure I hadn't lost her as she followed me. Once there, I had to park Paula's car in her one-stall garage. You know the kind, the typical apartment-garage stall with three inches to spare on all sides.

This was definitely NOT time for error in judgment No. 8!

I managed to get her car in with only two tries. I helped Paula carry her stuff into her place and asked her if she had enough ice. She said she did, and I was just turning to leave when I realized this was almost error in judgment No. 8. I forgot to say hello to Geordi! Neither Paula nor Geordi would have forgiven me for this lack of manners. So I went over to Geordi's cage and told him his Mommy had an accident and he was to be a nice, quiet bird and let Mommy rest. I told Paula that Jan and I were only a phone call away. Then, before anyone could bat an eye, "Fran has left the building."

I got into Jan's car. We immediately looked at each other and gave deep, deep sighs. You know, sometimes a sigh says a thousand words.

We left Paula's and went back to the church to retrieve my car, but not without first stopping to get something to eat. It didn't seem enough of a reward for the kind of afternoon we had been through, but then, we didn't have the headache Paula had.

Backword

Or whatever it is called when you want to add an update to The End. Since the beginning of the story is called a foreword, I figured this part must be called a backword.

I went to work the next morning surprised I hadn't gotten a phone call from Paula. I called her extension, and lo and behold, she answered! I told her how impressed I was she had come to work; I would have thought her too sore to even get out of bed. She said it wasn't easy, but she came. I asked her what her co-workers said when they saw her, she relayed that although she had talked to several face-to-face, no one had said anything.

Since her birthday was only a week later, I thought it only fitting to get her something to remind her of our "wonderful" road-rally day. So I got a blood red, Frisbee golf disk, wrapped it, and sent it to her.

The Moral Of The Story Is: If someone invites you to "X," and you reply, "What's X?" Your answer should be a firm, "No Thanks!"

What They Don't Tell You About Having A Heart Cath

Setting The Scene

Remember the movie *The Bucket List*? It's the one where two dying men each have lists of things they want to do before they meet their maker. Well, I too have a bucket list, but there's a catch – it is a reverse one. My list consists of medical procedures I hope to never have done to my body. I'm pretty sure I'm not the only medical professional with that type of reverse-bucket list.

So far I have had the misfortune of crossing off such great medical adventures as: colonoscopy (more than once), urisepsis (where you hear them read off your blood pressures and they are so low you can't believe you are conscious), cortisone injection in the heel, and an appendectomy at the age of fifty-eight. Then, of course, there was the naso-gastric tube they politely asked me to swallow.

This year, my health took a downward spiral. Suddenly I am crossing things off my bucket list I hadn't known existed: a 48-hour EEG where they glue all the leads to your head and send you home for two days, getting a phone call from your doctor's office telling you she wants you to make an appointment with a cardiologist immediately and having said cardiologist inform you that you need a heart catheterization done soon.

But this story is about the twist of fate that took place after the heart cath, revealing I had pulmonary hypertension. That twist led to a referral to a specialist in pulmonary hypertension. After meeting with him for two hours, he tells me he wants to do another heart cath – this one with an exercise component.

So sit back, eat your healthy apple and discover through my reverse-bucket list misadventure what they don't tell you about a heart cath. Hang on, it's a bumpy ride.

Five Hours Before The Cath

The procedure was scheduled for a Tuesday at 10:30 a.m. I would need someone to drive me there and back, and my wonderful, caring, helpful, considerate and bestest friend Jan volunteered. (Were those enough adjectives, Jan?) Unfortunately, the specialist was at a hospital about a ninety-minute drive from my house. So I set the alarm (didn't need to, wasn't really able to sleep anyway) and got up at six in the morning in preparation for the day.

Since I couldn't eat or even drink according to the pre-procedure instructions, an hour was plenty of time to be ready. Jan picked me up at seven and we headed down the interstate to the scene of my story. We got there precisely at 8:30 and I got myself checked in. Did you know that now they ask for a photo ID?

I was brought up to Room 202 in ODS (I'll give you a little time to interpret those initials). The check-in then began in earnest. I was given a basic hospital gown and told to change into it, but could leave on my socks and underpants. After doing as I was told, I sat down on the bed and discovered that sandpaper can disguise itself as a bed sheet. By the end of the day, my butt cheeks were definitely red and tender.

The nurse then started the IV in my left wrist. Here's a question for the nursing community: Why, in Florence Nightingale's name, do you think that using two needle sticks to start an IV is better than only one needle stick? You think you need to inject Novocain so the IV insertion is less painful, but you are trying to avoid pain by poking me with an extra needle. Thank you for listening, I've wanted to ask that for a long time.

By the way, anyone guess the riddle yet? ODS stands for One Day Stay!

After my IV torture concluded, the aide came in with an Accu-Chek to check my blood sugar. She said she, too, was diabetic, so I trustingly stuck out my finger. She went on to poke and prod, putting a drop on the Accu-Chek strip. Five seconds later, she relayed it hadn't worked and would have to do it over again. Fortunately, my finger was still bleeding, so she just started over with a new test strip. This time it was a success.

This should have signaled just how the day was going to be. My blood sugar had been 92 at home at 6 a.m. At 9 a.m., it had dropped to 79. Not a good sign.

The nurse went off to discuss this with Dr. S and came back with a syringe full of glucose, which she added right into the IV line. This led to me growing pretty warm at that point. Jan even reported my face turned beet red.

The IV bag was soon switched to dextrose while we waited. The procedure was to be at 10:30 a.m., so right on schedule they came for me at 11 a.m. Just as the nurse wheeled my bed and me into the hallway, I asked if I was still supposed to have my underpants on, as I had not been told to take them off. She said matter-of-factly that yes, they did have to come off. I then proceeded to make motions as if I was going to remove them, right then and there. That poor nurse got herself and the bed in reverse so fast, all the while asking me to wait until we were back in the room. That was fun.

Once back in the room, I slipped the suckers off, where they were neatly deposited in the closet. Then the journey started all over again.

The Prep

Those who know me well enough know that I am terrible with names. So even though they introduced themselves, I will refer to my nurses as Laverne and Shirley.

My bed was pushed over next to the cath table, which I gracefully scooted onto. Laverne unsnapped the top of my gown and proceeded to place a plethora of leads all over my chest, among various other locations not to be discussed here. She then placed a nasal cannula for oxygen on my face, because I never felt any oxygen coming directly up my nose. Did you notice where I said Laverne re-snapped my gown, or even placed it back where it had been? No, of course not.

While that was happening, Shirley raised my gown to expose my groin area. She had taken out the razor and proceeded to shave away "down there." Now, I need to explain something very important here: There is a general misconception on the location of the groin. It is not located on the upper leg. Do you get this? The groin is what's above the leg but below the navel – not exactly a distinction that comes up in normal, adult conversation.

Here is my warning to all you normally modest people out there, eating your butter burgers, setting yourselves up to go through this very same procedure: THERE IS NO PRIVACY IN THE CATH LAB! The only part of my anatomy covered by that wonderful hospital gown was my stomach.

The next step was something that had not been done during my first heart cath. Shirley, when done shaving, told me they were going to tape my stomach out of the way. Honest, that's exactly what she said, and that's exactly what they did. Getting out a large roll of white tape – probably 2 to 3 inches wide – she proceeded to shove my tummy up while attaching one end of the tape to the skin and passing the roll back to Laverne. She pulled the other end of the tape tightly and attached it to some part of the table. Then came another strip of tape. It was all very strange, and very embarrassing.

Wait a minute; I just realized I got a free tummy tuck! Temporary, but free.

Laverne and Shirley also had me turn my head to the left and scrubbed my neck in case Dr. S could not get the catheter started in that wonderful groin area. They placed a drape on my neck, so big it totally covered my face. Every once in a while, Laverne would lift it a little to see if I was still there.

The drape had another disadvantage. Numerous times during the procedure, either Laverne or Shirley would encourage me by telling me to take a couple of deep breaths. I wanted to inform them maybe if they took the %$^&* drape off my face, I wouldn't have that problem!

To conclude prep, Laverne injected a little medicine into my IV – just enough to relax, but enough that I knew what was going on. Dr. S arrived, and we finally got down to business.

The Procedure

Dr. S chatted with me a little, explained what was going to happen, and then off we went. He was so proud of himself, he told me later, because he got the catheter in on the first try. You can guess my opinion on that: Damn straight you had better have gotten it in on the first try!

Afterward was a jumble of moving fluoroscope, taking a reading on his command, and his moving the catheter to another area of my heart or pulmonary vessels. Then we efficiently moved on to part two. He called for the nitrous oxide, and Laverne placed a facemask over my mouth and told me to breathe deep. Now *that* is a relaxer, a real nice relaxer!

They did more of the same stuff, only to have Dr. S spoil the fun by having the nitrous oxide mask removed.

We had to wait a few minutes then for the fumes to clear before starting part three. Infamous part three, as in the reason I was lying on a cath table for the second time in four months. You see, part three is the exercise part. Dr. S wanted to replicate the exercise that would normally cause me to become so short of breath. Since they obviously couldn't let me off the table to climb a flight of stairs, they resorted to dumb bells.

Laverne got my left arm untangled from that white tape while Shirley took the blood pressure cuff off my right arm. I was told to stretch my arms out to the side while they placed a dumb bell in each hand and told me to start lifting up and down. Faster, faster, you fool, you fool! (I don't imagine that last little bit made much sense, but I had heard it in some movie and it has stuck with me.)

It took a long time. I must have good upper body strength. When I finished, I still didn't feel quite as winded as I get from climbing a flight of stairs, but pretty darn close. Dr. S said I could stop, and I did.

My first thoughts involved wanting someone to please come and get these dumb bells soon. They did take them away, eventually. Both Laverne and Shirley had been constantly commenting on how well I did and how long I lasted. Big deal, get me out of here.

Dr. S removed the catheter and left. The girls removed the drapes; a third nurse came and held a huge piece of gauze on the incision site. Then it was time to remove that white tummy tape. It was just slightly painful, with the tape being ripped from a very tender section of my body, but I tolerated it without screaming. The nurses discussed how they both had bad backs, so they called for backup. They slid a thin board under me. One, two, three – they got me back on my hospital bed. I still wasn't covered much, but they got me back together before I left the cath lab.

I had left the room at 11 a.m. and returned at approximately 1 p.m. Jan was there, waiting patiently as ever, reading a book.

And Now We Wait

One of the nurses was being extra helpful and asked if I would like a drink of water. She brought me some and even helped me drink it. As if on cue, another nurse came in and said I was not to have anything for an hour and a half. Oh well, it sure was good.

For that first hour, I slept. When I finally opened my eyes all the way, I chatted with Jan awhile, relaying all the details

I've just told you. A nurse came in to record my blood pressure. She reminded me that doctor's orders were for nothing by mouth for ninety minutes and flat in bed for two hours. Then you know what she did next? She snuck a peek under the covers! Come on now; get your mind out of the gutter. She was checking the incision site to make sure it wasn't bleeding.

It then became a matter of watching the clock and carrying on a conversation with Jan.

"You know, I can eat in thirty minutes. And in sixty minutes, I'm getting out of this bed."

Jan just nodded patiently. A short time later, I had another important announcement for her. "You know, I can eat in twenty-five minutes and in fifty-five minutes I'm getting out of this bed."

Jan informed me a few days later I had kept her informed about the timetable several more times after that ... several, several times.

Well, wouldn't you know it; the nurse came in again while I still had forty-five minutes left of lying flat. I didn't want to do it, I wouldn't do it, I had to do it – I asked for a bed pan! I knew I was willing to wait, but my bladder thought differently. So the nurse brought in a "real" bed pan, Jan stepped out and the bed pan was slid under my backside. I proceeded to tell the nurse she might as well get lost for a while; I have a very shy bladder.

Who among you noticed I described the bed pan as "real?" This goes back to my first heart cath. As the doctor was finishing up, he ordered 80 milligrams of Lasix to be added to my IV. I had barely made it back to my room before I really, *really* had to go. They graciously brought me a bed pan, the width and diameter of which was a little skimpy. The worst part, though, was it was not very deep at all.

So everyone left while I tried to release the floodgates. Without grossing out those of you who get upset when bodily functions are discussed, I will make two comments to summarize:

1) Lasix in an IV is a very powerful drug;

2) The nurses got a lot of practice emptying said bed pan.

With the urgent bodily function taken care of, the aide came in to take my food order, which turned out to basically be soup and a sandwich. I shoveled that down in record time. Then the aide came back with another hospital gown to wear as a robe so I could get up and walk. Hooray, I was finally set free!

I put on the gown and stood up from bed. The aide asked if I wanted my shoes. After a few awkward seconds, I realized she did not consider herself a cocker spaniel to be used for fetching the shoes. So I walked over to where they were and put them on – slip-ons, no tying involved. Then the aide left the room ... without me.

I pondered on that one a few seconds and asked Jan if she would like to take a walk. Cue Jan, IV pole and I walking up and down all four hallways of the ward before returning to the room. Once there, we waited ... and waited ... and waited ... until a nurse came in to say Dr. S would arrive in about ten minutes to talk. Again, we waited and waited. It got to the point where I wandered over to the doorway and poked my head outside. Not a soul in sight.

Jan suggested I just sit down and wait for the doctor, but by then I was way past impatient. I wanted to know what he found, and I wanted to get home!

So I took another stroll down toward the nurses' station. At first, I saw no one there, but then along came my favorite aide. I mentioned I was told Dr. S would be in to see me in ten minutes, and that ten minutes had been an hour and ten minutes ago. She kind of shrugged and kept on walking. Annoyed, I turned around and went back to my room.

Summary

When Dr. S finally arrived, we gathered around a paper he brought along. It was then he said those often-heard words: "I have good news and bad news."

The good news was the measurements he had taken were all much improved from those taken in January. The bad news was the measurements he took while I was exercising were much worse than even those from January. Basically, this equates to I'm okay until I move.

Now it is his turn to come up with a solution so I can climb a single flight of stairs and not be totally exhausted. As he left, I heard him exclaim, "My nurse will call you tomorrow and fill you in on any changes, etc." I then waited while the nurse removed the IV. I got dressed and let the aide take me down to the entrance in a wheelchair. Jan drove up and we were out of there. If you're curious, we drove off at 5:30 p.m., nine hours after we arrived and 11½ hours after our day began. Being a crackerjack mathematician, my final calculation, including the drive back with a meal stop on the way, our day was fourteen hours long. And how was your day?

As is usually the case, his nurse did not call me the next day even though I waited and waited and waited. The day after that, Thursday, his nurse did not call me even though I waited and waited and waited. The pattern was finally broken on Friday, but with an unforeseen twist.

Since I had not heard from Dr. S's nurse by Friday, I called the office at 9 a.m. and asked for an update. The update I received was his nurse was not in that day, but they would make sure one of the other nurses called me back. So I waited ... and waited ... and waited. At about 12:30 p.m., I got dizzy and weak, and ended up spending quality time in our own Urgent Care for two hours. Once out of Urgent Care – with no real explanation as to why my body rebelled on me – I took the time to phone Dr. S's office to check on my status there. Well, they were awfully busy, but someone would call. I told the person on the phone she should maybe point out to Dr. S that I had just spent two hours in Urgent Care.

So I waited ... and waited ... and waited. I ate my lunch and waited. I did some work for an hour and I waited. I called my friends Lou and Rob to come and take my car and me home (I bet you thought I was going to be my usual, dumb self and drive myself. Well, I'm not that dumb anymore). And I waited and waited and waited. Finally, at 5:55 p.m., Dr. S's office nurse called to say I would be starting on a new medication. But due to my visit to Urgent Care, I should call him on Monday and let him know how I was feeling.

And I stopped waiting.

Yoga Is A Four-Letter Word

Ancient History

This story is not *actually* ancient history. It took place a few years ago, give or take a lifetime or two. To write a story off of scribbled notes from that long ago is not going to be easy, but I'll try. I feel I owe it to all those skeptics out there and all those baby boomers.

This is how it came to be that I, Miss Couch Potato of 1974, 1975, 1980, 1985 and 1993, took up yoga. To establish the correct time frame, this momentous event took place in 1995 when I had been trying to find inner peace. You know, that tranquil feeling some people actually experience (such people did not work where I worked, that's for sure).

I was confused, crying out in an ocean of turmoil, angst incarnate and miserable, and didn't know how to get out of my funk. I had already tried Feldenkrais, which is another movement therapy. Now there is a program to make you wonder, "What did we just do?" as you're putting on your coat at the end of class.

Here's my really rusty memory: Feldenkrais is taught for people who have muscle pain or a poor sense of balance. The only thing I remember is it centers on learning how to lay on the floor in such a way that you can stand up with one fluid movement. Thankfully, we were never graded.

In talking with one of my trusted health care providers, it was suggested I try yoga. I asked him to repeat himself in case my ears were playing tricks on me. He said the same thing. I began to wonder if we were on the wrong sides of the desk, gesturing at my rotund body, inquiring if he was serious. Yes, he was very serious. Yoga would include meditation, learning to breathe correctly, and as a bonus, I would meet new people.

He recommended a yoga instructor and used the professional version of, "Try it, you'll like it." I mulled over this remarkable suggestion, and in a moment of total insanity, called the yoga center. I found they had a beginners' class that fit my schedule. What luck!

So I signed up and waited for the start of a new chapter in my life.

First Day Of Class

The yoga center was on the near east side of Green Bay, not an area I would usually frequent at night. The building was not hard to miss, though, with red and white siding striped horizontally. The class was held on the second floor. To get up there, you simply had to take the narrow, 80-degree-angle staircase up to the second floor. That is the most bizarre stairs I have seen. You're almost climbing straight up. I often wondered if I would fall backward if I ever were to stop in mid-flight. I chose not to find out.

At the top of the stairs, I traveled back in time to my college years. There was a beaded curtain in the doorway to the class area, wrapped in the distinct smell of incense. I followed my nose and entered the room behind beaded curtain number one. It was loft-like; one long, narrow room with wood floors and a very tall ceiling. There appeared to be a small area in one corner with black pillows and plants, all that "groovy" stuff. I guessed that area was for meditation.

Very promptly, the instructor arrived! I immediately started planning revenge on the person who had sent me here. The instructor's name was Dan, and he stood before me, about twenty-five years old, less than six feet in height, with a shaved head and wire-rimmed glasses. He was wearing the latest in yoga fashion, a type of oversized harem pants and a t-shirt with the sleeves ripped off.

Then there were the tattoos! He had a few of them, you could say; his whole left arm, right forearm, right middle finger, and both ankles covered. As the weeks went by, the tattoos on his ankles started to climb up his legs.

As we sat on the floor, like disciples to the teacher, we listened to Dan's introductory dissertation on yoga and the meaning of life. He took his yoga very seriously. We then were told to lie on the floor and breathe, as this was to relax us.

Dan taught us the proper yoga-breathing technique. At this point, in this position, with the quietness all around, I nearly fell asleep! But then we got up to work.

Dan informed us we were going to learn the sunrise salutation one pose at a time. Tonight's focus was to bend over with feet and hands flat on the floor. This is, of course, impossible for the average human being, but I pretended I was doing it correctly. I forget the name of this one, so I instead dubbed it the Hairpin.

After working on this for a while, we had to relax again. I remember thinking I could get into all this relaxing!

Next, we all sat on the floor in the traditional yoga position (I was not able to be traditional). Yoga-boy Dan was talking to us in that I-am-going-to-hypnotize-you tone. Just as I was drifting off, I heard a bell sound. It reminded me of the school play done at my high school, *Death of a Salesman* – the part way at the end when the salesman's widow does her soliloquy? The bell sounded two more times. Then Dan said, "Nice day, hold my candle," and the class responded in kind. Now, I know you find this quote hard to believe, but I swear with my right hand on a yoga mat, that is what he said. That's my story and I'm sticking to it.

Two Days Later, Class Two

I talked myself into returning to that room mostly because I wanted to make sure it was really there and not just an incense-induced dream. Surprisingly, the other students came back, too. We had even added three new students, but I was still twice as old as anyone else.

Two of the new students, two women, came together. They were an interesting couple. And by the end of the night I positively concluded it was not the lighting: both women had very hairy legs.

We started the same as the first time around, relaxing, breathing and that first pose. Then to move on, yoga boy had us gather in a circle and taught us three-step deep breathing. As we practiced, he moved around and listened to everyone's breathing one-by-one, giving pointers. He told me I did well, in case you were curious.

We then learned a new pose, the Downward Dog. Don't ask me why it's called that; to this day I have no idea. I called it "See My Butt."

We all begin on our hands and knees, but this is not the pose. Oh no ... this is only the starting point. We then lift off of our knees and balance on our toes, with our backs straight. Oh, why did I come? I am insane. I truly couldn't do it. I tried and I tried, but I just couldn't do it! I couldn't even do just one!

I was trying my best, sweating profusely in the effort (this is where I resolved to bring a sweat rag to each class), when yoga boy approached. I looked at him and said, "I don't know which muscles to tell to move!" Finally, I cheated and did only one leg at a time.

But the torture was not over. We went on to the Straddle Pose. The Straddle pose consists of jumping from Downward Dog and ending up with your feet in opposite directions, trunk facing forward, and then reaching sideways and bending down the leg on that side. We held that position much longer than necessary, then switched and bent onto the other side. The only way I can describe this pose is to compare it to the wall drawings in the pyramids; you know, the "walk like an Egyptian."

I have since come to understand the workout – and pain – of yoga is not the position into which you are contorted, but rather the length of time you are expected to stay in that position.

We were mercifully done then, except for the rest at the end. But tonight we did it a little differently. Lying on the floor, yoga boy wanted us to rest with our butts against the wall and our legs stuck straight up against it. He explained that next class we would be doing shoulder stands, so this would be a good introduction.

What? Shoulder stands? In your dreams, yoga boy, but definitely not in mine! Then it was, "Nice day, hold my candle," and we were out of there.

On the way out, I noticed something I hadn't noticed the first time. Along the walls there were red ropes attached with bolts. I grew a little concerned, wondering when we would be using those.

Day Three - The Midpoint

There were only three of us students that night, as the hairy-leg girls didn't show. And so class starts like the previous ones: rest, breathe, repeat, Downward Dog and Straddle pose. This time, I did the dog without cheating.

Day three's new pose involved bending up and down at the waist, following by ups and downs with hands on floor. I got this part first try. Then we locked fingers behind our backs, bent down again, and lifted our arms toward the ceiling. I don't remember the yoga name for this one, but I suspect it is the Human Anchor.

The next new pose was the Warrior. This guy begins with the back foot planted east and the front foot planted west. We then twisted our trunk north and slightly bent the front knee. To top it off with a dramatic twist, we raised our arms out to the side and turned our heads west, opposite of the twist of the trunk. The whole thing seemed more like the Human Pretzel to me, or a mad version of Mapquest.

Finally, the pose we have all been waiting for: the Shoulder Stand. We practiced this against the wall first. Lying on our backs and scooting our butts as close to the wall as possible, we then inserted several folded blankets to give us a butt-head start. Then, we raised our legs so they were flat against the wall. We were to put our hands behind our backs, just at the waist, and push to raise our bodies farther up the wall.

This is the point where you must make a critical decision: Do you wish to continue in this tenuous position, or do you want to breathe? Because my bodily organs were now all crammed into my chest cavity and there was really not adequate room for my lungs, I opted for oxygen. After several futile attempts, yoga boy suggests I rest quietly while the others continue their own personal struggles.

That was it for the night, thank goodness! We did our resting. This time, yoga boy offered us lavender-scented eye bags and/or stomach stones. He explained the stones were good if you lay them on your lower abdomen, as they move while you are breathing and are good for the uterus. Oh no, more information than I need, young man! Then it was, "Nice day, hold my candle," and we were out of there.

Day Four - We Put It All Together

This night, we were going to put together all the poses we had learned so far, complete with the Sun Salutation. Yoga boy was showing off his new tattoos, wearing some awful print shorts so we could see his legs, of course. The new tattoo area had been shaved and looked rather red, in my medical opinion.

He showed us how to put the poses together, although he had forgotten to string a couple of the necessary poses in the middle. I chalk up his forgetfulness to all those gongs going off too close to his head. We then did three sequences of the Sun Salutation. I managed to hang in there for the first two.

Next were some more new poses with partners. We began by sitting on each other, doing the pose known as the Cobra. One of the pair goes into the Cobra position, which involves lying on your stomach and lifting your head and trunk off the floor. The other partner helps by sitting on the cobra's calves and pulling back on the cobra's hand. Then you get even by changing positions. My name for this one was the Rack.

We then did more dogs and more shoulder stands. My anatomy hadn't changed in two days, so I was again unsuccessful in raising my butt. By that time, we were done for the night, so we got into rest position. Perhaps in honor of his new tattoos, yoga boy hit a gong, again and again and again and again.

Nice day, hold my candle.

Day Five – Yoga Boy Shows Off

There are only three students again. We review the Sun Salutation, doing three sequences. Yoga boy subtly suggests that if anyone gets tired, they should rest in the Child's Pose. I took his challenge and kept up through all the sequences. Oh yes, when you're good, you're good and sweaty. Then we moved on to some new poses.

First is the Cobbler. This one is done sitting on the floor with your legs straight out in front of you. Then you grab your feet, the big toe if you can get there, and fold forward. Yoga boy can do this and get his torso all the way to the floor. We straddle our legs out and fold forward as best we can with him. Again, he gets all the way to the floor. Those new tattoos must have healed fast.

The next set of poses started out with us on our hands and knees. We bring our right foot forward and bend it at the knee, so the leg is just under you. Then, we stretched the other leg as far back behind as it could go. This is the Backward Prayer pose, but I called it Mission Impossible.

There are other versions of Mission Impossible. The first is to reach back and grasp your elbows and fold forward. The other one is quite impressive, as you reach back for your left foot and pull it up. To achieve the third and final variation, you bring both arms over your shoulders to grab the foot and pull it up. At this point, I changed my opinion of yoga boy. I thought he was double-jointed, but he's not – he's quadruple-jointed!

Next came versions on the Warrior pose and practicing the shoulder stand. By now, we were not allowed the support of the wall. As yoga boy passed through the class, he tells me to get my elbows under my back, not outside. What could I say, "The mind is willing, but the body is broke?"

Yoga boy did more showing off with different poses, and then rest period arrived. That infernal gong scared me again just as I was falling asleep.

Nice day, hold my candle.

Day Six - Graduation

By now, I had made a chiropractor's appointment for the following day, as my body was definitely broken. There were four of us here for the final class. We do the usual startups, and then try a pose requiring an extra joint between the wrist and elbow. Next were four sequences of Sun Salutation. Of course I kept up, but I needed a bucket to wring out my sweat rag.

Our next circus stunt – I mean, yoga stunt – began by sitting on the floor with knees bent and feet flat. We were supposed to make like a rocking horse and slowly, vertebrae by vertebrae, roll back while continuing to rock. My attempt was just a big thump, as I evidently have only one vertebra. I was looking about as stupid as all of the first five classes put together, so yoga boy came over and stepped on my feet. You may think this was a cruel gesture, but it actually helped me rock back and forth just like the others. Well, sort of. Actually, there were three rocking horses and one glue-factory reject.

We did some partner poses again. I felt so sorry for my partner. I knew at the end our differences in "height" hadn't hurt her, but she had to be shaking in her shorts. There were two different poses tried; not mastered by any means, but we gave it a good go.

For the sake of clarity, the first person was Red and the second person was Blue. Pose one involved Red kneeling so close to the wall she could kiss it. Blue lies on the floor behind and puts one foot on the base of Red's spine and the other foot between the shoulder blades. Then Red simply lengthens her spine and bends back, *way* back. I called this one Timber.

The other pose was a disaster waiting to happen. When yoga boy told us this next step, we all just stared at him and thought his mind had been addled by all that tattoo ink. Red was to kneel in Child's Pose. Blue stands with her back to Red. Then she simply lowers herself onto Red's back, butt first. Both have their hands above their heads and grasp each other's hands and slowly match each other's breathing. The weight of Blue is evenly distributed and causes no problem for Red, and it's actually quite comfortable. And yes, we all did both parts. This one I named Yoga Pile.

We finished by perfecting our shoulder stands. Let me rephrase that: The other three students worked on their shoulder stands. Yoga boy and I had come to a mutual understanding about my few strong areas and my many shortcomings. I looked at him with a "no way" look on my face, and he just nodded and walked away.

Afterward was rest time, complete with gongs and – you guessed it – nice day, hold my candle.

Alright, send up the rockets, I made it! I actually finished the yoga class. I was amazed and proud of myself, as I had actually enjoyed it. I even considered signing up for another beginners' class.

There really were so many advantages, better breathing, better posture, better strength and better flexibility. Yet even after all that, I quickly changed my mind. The plus sides were impressive, but the minuses far outweighed them. What were these down sides, you ask? Pain, pain, pain, pain, and pain.

As far as I'm concerned, "been there, done that."

You've Got To Be Kidding, My Body Is Not Made That Way!

For you to really grasp what a stretch this was, you need to know how fit I am …. NOT!

In high school, my best friend was a girl named Sandy. We did everything together and managed to be in physical education at the same time. One of the sections of the class was tumbling (in future years, it became known as gymnastics floor exercise). Anyway, we spent a few weeks learning certain tumbling, acrobatic moves and positions. These classes were held in the boys' wrestling practice room, as the floor was covered with cushioned mats.

Well, Sandy and I were not too fond of this class section, and we certainly were not in the least bit capable of completing any of the required moves. As a result, we tried to take ourselves out of our gym teacher's sight by taking over the back corner mat. We aptly named it the "Dummy Mat." If anyone else in the class wanted to come over onto our mat, they were welcome. But, if they were able to do a headstand or any of the required tricks, they were immediately asked to leave. It was only for dummies, like Sandy and me, who couldn't even sit with our legs crossed, much less complete a headstand.

What Am I Doing Here?

I was feeling pressured by several loving family members, friends and demanding health care providers to "get in shape." But I can procrastinate with the best of them, and I had gotten my 58-year-old body this far without any wellness adjustments at all. I didn't mind, but just to quiet down all those other voices, I started considering maybe doing something healthy for my body. Mind you, I was only considering doing *something*.

Then fate stepped in, going by the name of Dana (which I decided stood for Do Another Ninety Ab-stretches). My employer decided to take the health of its employees to the next level. They offered a Women's Wellness Club, with Dana as the instructor (translated: workout maniac).

So for six weeks, two nights a week, we went to the Ashwaubenon clinic site's Core Performance Center to exercise. And boy, did we exercise HARD! Each night we are there, just when we thought there was nothing she could possibly think of to break our bodies further, Dana comes up with another variation of an already impossible exercise.

We were weighed and measured at the first session. Now, I can understand the waist and butt, but they also measured our neck, shoulders, upper arms, thighs and calves. I'll jump ahead here and tell you my results after the first six weeks: I lost five pounds, but I also lost a total of sixteen – count them – sixteen inches. I lost an inch-and-a-half from my neck alone! The biggest loss, though, goes to my hips, with a whopping five inches gone.

The members of the group I exercise with are quite diverse, with one or two as out of shape as me and a few who aren't hopeless, but are there to avoid the decline in body condition looming just around the calendar. Then there are one or two others who would make me very envious if I could breathe enough to express envy. One woman in particular is in a league all her own. I know Dana is often challenged to find ways to adapt the exercises to my poor body condition, but I think she is probably equally challenged finding ways to make the exercises vigorous enough to make the in-shape woman sweat like the rest of us.

Here are some of Dana's more infamous exercises:

Stretch bands – What she doesn't tell you initially is the reason for the different colors of these harmless-looking elastic bands. They're not colored to make them pretty. Oh no, the colors stand for how hard they are to stretch. The first week began with yellow, a piece of cake. Next up was the green. A little stiff, but not bad. And last week, but certainly not least, Dana pulled out the blue. I don't ever want to see the next color after blue.

Yellow Bands – Simple in that you place them around your ankles, but not so simple for the exercise-challenged. The first time I slipped on the band, I ended up twisting it into a figure 8.

Green Bands – Used most often for doing side-steps. By the end of your stepping, however, you definitely know you've been working some newly discovered muscles

Blue Bands – What a surprise, they have no stretch at all, or at least that's what they feel like. I put them on my ankles and I learned just how painful side-stepping can be.

Blue, plastic step boxes – The ones you see in all the aerobics classes. Here are some of Dana's variations:

Many times, it is one of the exercise stations and you simply do whatever you want as long as you keep moving on and off the box. Now, most people get very ambitious, while I have to pace myself so a simple step up, up, down, down, is enough for me.

One infamous day, Dana stacked up two boxes, and we had to do the step-up-step-down on twice the height. No big deal, right? Well, not exactly. Not that easy for someone with naturally short legs, stepping up that high and back down that far. It gradually wore hard on the hips after just ten or twelve seconds – and we had to go for a whole minute.

She then combined the steps and cones into one exercise, with the steps stacked two high, of course. The object was to push the stack of steps all the way across the room, circle the cone and head back across the floor. No problem, I thought, until I tried it! Bending over the box to place my hands on the stacked boxes wasn't too bad until you went a few feet. I was huffing and puffing and watching the floor to make sure I didn't run anybody over. By the time I got back to the starting point, Dana came to my rescue. She put one more step on top and said to give it a try. It went much better after that. I think there was a bit more space in my chest cavity for my lungs to expand.

The DPI – I can't wait anymore. I have to tell you about the most unusual exercise equipment experienced so far. Dana calls it something along the lines of a "Bosu Ball." I, however, have named it something else. The name I use fits the description perfectly. You see, this ball is actually an upper portion of a blue, gel-filled ball with a flat bottom, as if someone cut an exercise ball in half. It is about fifteen inches across and eight inches high. Now, if you have a visual of this, you've already guessed what I call it. That's right; it's a "Dolly Parton Implant!" For the sake of brevity, I will from now on call it "the DPI." Dana got very original with the DPI, and continues to do so.

The first time we saw the DPI, we were to use it to do pushups, positioning ourselves on the mat to line up our chest with Dolly's. That ensured we didn't have to bend down as far, and for some of the others, it was a help in bouncing yourself back up to the starting position.

Another time, we did pushups with them, but the DPI was flat side up. We had to position our hands on the surface and do the pushups. Here's the catch, however. The round, gel-side was now on the floor, making the whole exercise not one of strengthening the arms, but of testing our balance.

An earlier exercise we did started out by simply sitting on the thing. We were then to arch back and tighten our back and stomach muscles. It's not a position I can hold for a very long time, but at least I try.

Here comes the real corker. The object of this exercise is to do dumbbell punches while STANDING on the DPI! My first time at that position, I worked very hard on the balancing portion. Dana came by and said I could do the dumbbells, but from the floor and not from the DPI. I told her I would conquer the ball and balance on it – and I did! Then, I had to move on to the second phase of the routine. While gingerly standing on the DPI, I lifted one of the dumbbells about an inch. Let me tell you, the very next second I was standing on the floor. At least I didn't actually take a tumble and fall. I simply stepped off the DPI and chose to do the dumbbell exercise from the floor level ... that's my story, and I'm sticking to it.

Here's an example of an exercise gone very wrong. We start with the DPI on one end of a blue mat. Step one is to sit on the DPI. Step two, slide backward off the DPI. Step three has you lie back on the mat, followed by step four, placing both feet back on the DPI. With step five, you lift your butt off the mat, followed by step six, raising one foot off the DPI while straightening that leg and not allowing your butt to go back down. Finally, the torture ends with step seven, where one returns that lifted foot to the DPI and does the same with the other. I tried; I got as far as step three and had to quit and wait for Dana. I've since learned to watch the person in rotation ahead of me.

Large exercise ball – There are several sizes of these depending on the exercise. The size most often used is about three feet high.

Here's an easy one: To give a person a false sense of success, you simply sit on the ball while holding a pair of dumbbells. The gist is to sit on the ball and do dumbbell punches. Sounds very simple, unless you get cocky, pick up speed and find yourself with one leg and one arm flailing in the air, trying not to fall off.

Lean with your back against the wall and place the large ball between you and that wall, at about the level of the small of your back. The exercise calls for you to place your feet firmly a little in front of you and squat down, remaining as long as possible in that position. I, of course, can always sneak a break from the excruciating pain and stand up when Dana has her back turned.

Let's put a twist on that last one. Assume the position, but this time place your feet even more out in front of you. Then lift one foot and move it backward until the heel is touching the wall. Now you simply squat down, bending the knee forward.

Those are pieces of cake, you say? Now, assume the position, grab a five-pound medicine ball, and squat down. Oh yes, about that ball. While in the squat position, raise the ball above your head, bring it down between your knees and continue this routine until sweat rolls in your eyes and temporarily blinds you.

Here's a very recent large-ball exercise. Hint: It violates the four-step rule. First, kneel on the floor so your feet are flat against the wall behind you. Next, place the large ball in front of you and align it to your lower abdomen. Step three consists of leaning into the ball, raising your knees off the floor until step four takes over. While lifting your knees, roll up and forward on the ball.

In this ridiculous position, move on to step five by raising your hands above your head. Then lower your hands to touch the floor to round out step six. If you can, repeat steps five and six. Step seven is particularly important, so pay close attention: pray. Pray you can survive this exercise. (Yes, I did literally offer up a quick prayer – out loud – that I survive this particular nightmare.)

Hand Weights – They come in many different weights. Sometimes they are used for sit-ups. Dana places a couple of forty-pound weights at the far end of a blue mat, and you are supposed to slip your feet under these weights to help you do the sit-ups. The first time I tried that, my feet kept cramping up every time I jammed my feet under the bar of the weights. I've since worked my way into doing this without the cramps – yay! But then again, it doesn't really matter since I can't actually sit up while doing sit-ups anyway.

Each session, we do hand weights, Dana has us raising them in different directions depending on which muscles she wants us to work. I asked her once why, with all these weight-lifting exercises I keep doing, do my arms still shake while trying to do push-ups?

There's even a hand weight with a handle. It's a ball with a curved handle attached, shaped rather like a "J." We each kneel one knee on a bench. and then lift and lower this handled weight for full affect.

Now, here is a secret that leaked out one day. The weights they use there at the exercise classes are somehow magical. Really, magical! Because, after every fifteen to twenty seconds of an exercise, each weight gains one pound. Okay, maybe I'm only exaggerating. It just seems that way.

Yes, there are treadmills, and Dana finds ways to use them in the circuit each exercise night. There's nothing special about them. And someday, when I'm on one of them, I may even turn up the speed and actually jog! As of right now, however, I have to rush a little more quickly when I am moving onto the treadmill portion of the workout. I have to do this so I can get around to the left side of the control panel. No matter who I follow, I have to turn down the speed, sometimes quite a bit.

There is one exercise we did the very first session that Dana likes to re-visit again and again, like a rich relative. It begins with you lying on a blue mat. There is an orange hoop, like a flattened hula hoop, that you hold over your head like a steering wheel. Then you raise your legs, reach forward with the hoop, move the hoop over your feet, down your legs and back up again. I obviously have legs that are too long. Even though we do that particular exercise at least once a week, that orange ring has yet to see the soles of my shoes.

Here's our little secret: Sometimes I cheat on the exercises.

There is one Dana has had us do a few different times. Starting at the far end of the room, we jog across, climb the stairs leading up to the ground floor level, turn around and jog back down the steps, going all the way back to the far end of the room. Now, I may climb the stairs halfway, sit down, keep breathing and then stand up and return to the starting point.

There are other exercises I don't do at all because I physically can't, not because I don't want to. And I will proudly admit I can do more now than I could those first couple of weeks.

And Then it Was Gardening Season

Nothing trumps flower gardening on my list of priorities. So after the second six-week session with Dana, planting season was upon us and I was out of there. I had accomplished a lot, I really had! I am forever grateful for the opportunity to take off a few pounds and inches in the privacy of a room full of only women. But I am much more fit for gardening.

Remember that exercise I described with the orange ring? Well, I proudly report that the last time Dana had us doing that exercise, I *did* get the ring over my feet and legs, all the way back up again!

Now, I must sadly report I am writing this last section almost three years after the fact. Due to this, I suppose I cannot accurately report how much weight or inches I did lose in those weeks of torture. I do remember I lost more inches than pounds. And I also remember the number was more than twenty but definitely less than fifty. You make the final guess. I, of course, vote for forty-nine pounds and inches.

Epilogue

Dana must have rubbed off on me a little. I never went back to the women's wellness club, but I did become a member of a local fitness club. You just never know what twists and turns your life will take, especially if you have to do it using the blue bands.

Just Left Of Center

How I Spent My Summer Vacation

The start of my story begins with the innocent words: "I know ... I'll have an adventure. I'll go to Anaheim by Amtrak!" I knew this was going to be the year I went to my first national American Society for Clinical Laboratory Science convention. Since I was on the board of the state professional society, I was expected to attend the national convention as a delegate. The good news was this year's convention met in Disneyland. The bad news? Disneyland is in Anaheim ... Anaheim, California. That's a long way from my residence in Green Bay, Wisconsin.

Now, I have flown many times before. But my vacation last year included turbulence over Minneapolis, which taught me I am not quite ready to meet my maker! So I had to come up with Plan B.

At first it was a joke, going by train. But the more I thought about it, the idea didn't sound so dumb after all. I got more details about traveling by Amtrak through the mail. I could indeed get to Anaheim, but the journey would take two days each way. Oh well, I had plenty of vacation time coming.

So I made the reservations with the help of fellow board member, Cindy. I would leave from Milwaukee on Saturday at noon and arrive in Anaheim early Monday morning. After attending the convention from Tuesday to Saturday, I would leave Anaheim Saturday night and get back to Milwaukee early Monday evening the following week. Ten days of fun, sun, education, Mickey Mouse and new friends.

The following pages are an expanded version of the little notebook I wrote in daily during my trip. I hope you enjoy the amusing anecdotes from my travel journal. I did say I wanted an adventure, and I believe I succeeded.

Boy, did I succeed!

The Trip To California – To Explore Strange New Worlds

D-Day Minus One

I prepared very carefully for my trip. After all, I am a seasoned traveler and can pack in minutes if I have to. However, someone must have been playing with my watch, because I didn't finish packing until 10:30 that Friday night. At least I had already made the necessary purchases prior to

Friday: traveler's checks, cash, snacks, meds, and of course, essential reading materials. I still don't know what took so long to pack the rest of my things. Was it sorting through my jewelry armoire or chasing my cat, George, out of my suitcase several times? Maybe it was the half hour I spent in each of my two closets.

I did manage to put back three items of clothing I initially packed. I also determined I could get by with only four books. By the time I finally made it to bed a little past 10:30 p.m., visions of train schedules were dancing in my head.

D-Day: Saturday

At 6:30 a.m., I got myself ready, closed my suitcase and was actually on the road by 8:45, right on schedule. I took I-43 to Milwaukee, and yes, I did miss the turnoff again, backtracking onto I-94. I then parked my car in a locked lot across from the Amtrak station for a mere $3.00/day–pre-paid, of course.

Using one of my best purchases, a wheeled luggage rack (a must for traveling), I hauled my luggage across the street to the Amtrak station only to find I could not check my luggage until I got to Chicago. Hauling my biggest suitcase up the train steps and down the aisle was no picnic.

Two stops on the way down, and I arrived in Chicago right on time. Chicago's Union Station is big, BIG, B-I-G! They have screens on the walls with departures and arrivals just like airports. What they don't have are covered arrival gates and walkways leading the short distance to the terminal. Instead, Amtrak has you haul your luggage down those same steps you had so much fun climbing, to be greeted by all the big, noisy, hot, smelly, dirty trains. You get to pick up your luggage and stumble the whole length of the train, up a steep ramp (or down a steep ramp as the case may be) and stagger into Union Station.

Union Station is a world unto itself. Huge and very old, you feel you have just stepped into a 60-year time warp. That is, until you pass the first teenager, complete with tri-color hair, headphones, and clothes that look like they came from the Salvation Army. This is a built-in reality check, sure to confuse the weary traveler. I, on the other hand, was just starting my journey.

So I checked my large suitcase, adjusted my carry-on correctly over the wheels of the luggage rack, and set out to explore. I navigated the escalator with my luggage and found a mini-food court on the second floor, complete with ... McDonald's. I did stop at a bakery to grab a pastry for a late-night snack. Eventually, I wandered downstairs, found the appropriate waiting area, and – you guessed it – waited!

Boarding began about fifteen minutes before departure time. I later figured there had to be some kind of method to the madness.

There were roughly twenty cars to the train. The one dining and lounge car were centrally located. Those lucky travelers going the farthest distance, (for example, me) were seated in the car directly in front of the lounge. As each of us entered (or rather, mounted) the train, a car attendant assigned us seats. This also turned out to be a very tricky method. They must find compatible strangers to share their seat row with, as well as separate the families from the less tolerant passengers (me again). The Boy Scouts got a car pretty much to themselves.

This seating process quickly turned into my first rude awakening. I was assigned an aisle seat. In all of my air travels, I have graciously – and thankfully – taken aisle seats. I did NOT want to look out the window of a plane! For this trip, however, I felt I had earned a window seat.
Yet, I did not get a window seat. I got an aisle seat. Do you get the drift?

To say the least, I was not pleased with my seat assignment. The problem with aisle seats, as I was to learn, is there is nothing to lean against when trying to sleep, especially if you are traveling alone.

I was lucky in that my seat partner, who got the window seat I so dearly craved, was a seasoned Amtrak traveler. In that first hour, she filled me in on all the finer points of train travel. All of the coach cars (that means just seats, no beds) are two stories. There are about twenty seats on the first level for those who have trouble getting around, and about seventy seats on the second level. My seat was about two-thirds back, across from the bottled-water dispenser – a water dispenser some of the less-disciplined children found to be a tempting plaything.

Description time on some of my fellow passengers: My seat partner, Kathy, was about ten years older than me. From a Chicago suburb, her son had bought her a plane ticket, but she chickened out at the last minute, opting to buy a train ticket instead. She was heading to Los Angeles to visit her children.

The young man in front of us started talking to us right away. He was upset because he had missed his train for the northern route and Amtrak had re-routed him on ours. He was pretty vocal, and incidentally, let us know he was also homeless. I didn't quite understand that claim. If he was homeless, where did he get the money for the train ticket?

The man was sporting an interesting hairstyle, a shaved head except for a short, saucer-sized patch at the crown and another short patch near the bottom middle part of his head the size of a silver dollar.

Our young friend did not stay in his seat very much during the trip. In my wanderings, I found him imparting his vast store of knowledge and wisdom to anyone he could corner – excuse me – chat with.

The two men across from me were complete strangers, yet talked constantly about common interests: music, jazz, guitars. The woman behind me was constantly mumbling to herself. At least, so I thought, until I turned around the second day and found her dictating into her video camera, recording the view from her window seat.

When we stopped about 10 p.m. (we stopped for passengers a total of about twenty times during the trip), a woman got on and was assigned the aisle seat in front of me. Since the Bald One was still off wandering, she immediately pulled out the pillow she brought along and went to sleep across both seats. She then proceeded to cough…and cough…and cough…and cough. I dubbed her Typhoid Mary. TB ward, here I come!

But more about Typhoid Mary later. They turned down the overhead lights around 10 p.m., so I settled down for some sleep. I didn't get much of it, let me tell you. Lots of germs, but not much sleep.

I thought I could sleep in a recliner. But as you remember, I had as aisle seat, and could not lean against anything or lie on my side. The seat's back reclined to less than a 45-degree angle, with foot rests that are supposed to line up the upper leg to the knee – that is, if you can get them up. There is no control to raise the leg rest, only to lower it. So you must reach down, grab the leg rest, move your legs out of your way and then lift the leg rest. Sounds simple, right? In reality, it can't be done!

Luckily, Kathy showed me the trick. You get up, raise the leg rest, and jump back into your seat. Awkward, but effective. Goodnight to day one.

D-Day Plus One: Sunday

I woke around 6 a.m. and went down to attend to my toilet. I soon learned to use the handicapped facilities, as they're the only ones you can turn around in or move into any other essential positions required in a bathroom. The other toilets were so narrow you had to back into them, and definitely not wide enough for the aforementioned positions. So I washed my face, brushed my teeth and combed my limp hair.

I got back to my seat and watched the countryside roll by as I ate the breakfast I had brought along. Yes, Toto, we are in Kansas! I then took the first of many naps.

After awakening, I went back to the snack bar in the observation car to buy a ham and cheese sandwich and Coke. In the observation car, the windows wrap around the top and the seats can be adjusted to face directly out.

I should first explain the operation of moving from one car to another. It's a precarious little dance. As you get up from your seat, you face the direction you are headed and walk/sway to the end of the car, hanging onto the seat backs whenever the seas (oops, that's my cruise experience coming through) rails get too rough. At the end of each car is a metal door with a window and a black rectangle that says "Press." When you press the press bar, the door slides sideways and you advance into the space between the two cars. Here the swaying is more obvious as you look down and see the metal plates at your feet moving in opposite directions. You step onto these metal plates and press the press bar for the car you are entering, and step across into it. The doors close automatically behind you. It's an easy task for a seasoned cruise traveler or a habitual drinker.

My seatmate Kathy and I decided to have dinner in the dining car. This meant we had to make reservations with the maître-d' as he came through the cars. When it came time for our reservation, we walked back to the dining car and were seated at a linen-covered table with crystal, silver and fine china.

Of course, by this time I have been in the same clothes and stringy hairdo for far too long, and felt as if I'd be thrown out at any minute. Why do they set such a fancy table? We all would be happy with a plain table with paper plates and plastic forks.

But I must say, the meal lived up to its setting. I had honey lemon chicken, rice, veggies and dessert for $11.95 plus tip. We finished dinner as we pulled into Albuquerque, New Mexico. This is the only stop on the trip with enough time for passengers to get off the train. We stayed about forty minutes, enough for us to check out the native-jewelry sale tables that just happened to be there and open. I managed to find a hat pin for my collection. The stop really didn't make sense, since we were already an hour behind schedule. But you can't deny commerce.

I finally figured out a group of travelers seated on the lower level of our car. It was a group of young teenage girls. One of them was a little person. They all spent their time going up and down the stairs to go back to the observation car. I finally realized that the little person was not changing clothes that often. She was twins!

Now, an update on Typhoid Mary. When the Bald One came by and saw he had lost his seat to Typhoid Mary, he grew concerned. He asked her how she was and she coughed something back, which is when he took it upon himself to search for the conductor. The conductor came back to talk to "Mary" and suggested she be checked by paramedics, as she really did not look well. How's that for an understatement?

We arrived in Flagstaff, Arizona, after dark and were met at the train station by a fire truck and ambulance. Four paramedics came on and talked with "Mary," checking her vital signs and taking some of her medical history. I overheard bits and pieces like a blood oxygen content of 84 percent (normal is about 99 percent), bronchitis, asthma and half of a lung gone. The paramedics tried real hard to get her to come with them to the hospital, but she wasn't having any of that. She was going to her daughter's in San Bernardino, and that was that.

So the paramedics had her sign a release, left the train and the train left Flagstaff. Needless to say, it was just as well I couldn't sleep that night. I spent the hours trying to get comfortable, hearing Typhoid Mary cough (at least that meant she was still alive) and wondering what the incubation period for TB was.

D-Day Plus Two, Monday

I awoke at 6 a.m. and washed up for the day. Before you work up too much pity, that's 6 a.m. Pacific Time, 8 a.m. Central Time. Really had you thinking I was an early bird, didn't I?

Unfortunately, we were now two hours behind and would be arriving in Los Angeles at 9:30 a.m. You find when riding trains that more often than not, their tracks go through some of the worst parts of town that just about any path can cut through. Los Angeles is no exception. I saw homeless people washing their clothes in the overflow conduits; their little shacks made of old boxes, palm fronds and discarded furniture. Always a cheery sight as a visitor enters a city.

The Los Angeles Union Station actually looked older than the one in Chicago, but not as large. I got my luggage from baggage claim, found the gate for the shuttle train to Anaheim, and sat employing my favorite pastime: people watching. The supply was generous and varied. Among my observations were the train station employees, who, when they were boarding their shuttle, employed one of their own favorite activities: human stampeding. They ran passengers at a brisk trot with full suitcases down two long corridors, across a steep ramp corridor and outside, with a climb into the train and passengers carrying all their luggage. The station employees offered no help.

The train in question started up and proceeded to its first stop, Fullerton, where incidentally my train stopped on the way into L.A. It was an extra extension of the trip I planned to avoid on my way back home. I would ride from Anaheim to Fullerton and wait there for my train to Chicago.

We finally arrived in Anaheim at about 11:30 a.m., where I called a cab to take me to my hotel, the Disneyland Hotel. Mickey, here I come!

The Anaheim Experience – Beam Me Up, Scotty

Day One, Monday

My taxi ride to the Disneyland Hotel made me wonder why I had even bothered to avoid the trauma of a plane ride. I hadn't avoided the gut-wrenching feel of free-fall at all. There was no fanfare of trumpets announcing my arrival, so with a slightly disappointed edge, I gathered my luggage on my handy-dandy luggage cart and went in search of the registration desk.

Checking in was complicated by the fact that of the three persons registered for our room, my name was not listed, and the room was under Cindy's name and credit card. To get a bed to sleep in that first night, I had to sacrifice one of my own credit cards. Hopefully Cindy would be able to straighten out this mess later in the week or I was going to have a whopper of a credit card bill next time.

The next catch was they'd take my credit card, but couldn't give me a room key. Rooms would not be available until 3 p.m., sorry. So I had to sit in the lobby for three hours, with three-day-old greasy hair and three-day-old clothes. I didn't even want to be near me!

I sat for a while to gather my wits – some of which were hard to find. I decided not to waste my time sitting, since this is what I had mostly been doing for the past two days. Instead, I opted to locate the convention registration booth and pick up my registration packet.

Dkfal;dfj[glda

(Sorry about that, my cat, George, just decided to help me with my typing.)

The packet consisted of a canvas bag, a nametag with plastic holder, string for the holder, a credit card with your name and address (more about this magical item later) and another rectangular plastic case for which no one ever discovered its use. Convention attendees could acquire a weeklong, no limits pass for the unbelievable price of $26.00. So of course, I bought one.

The long-anticipated 3 p.m. finally arrived and I received my room key for Room 2433, on the sixth floor. I never did figure out the numbering system. The room was spacious, with two double beds and a pullout sofa. There was the usual TV and stocked refreshment center with such items as peanuts for $1.75, soda and beer for $2.50 and a deck of cards for $3.00. I, however, resisted the temptation to raid the refrigerator. Even though I was cat-tired (anyone who has been owned by a cat knows they take tired to a finer art form), I still managed to unpack and shower off my travel dirt. I intended to take a long nap, possibly until the next morning, but, drat, I was over-tired and couldn't sleep. So I changed into party clothes, grabbed my D-land ticket and headed for the monorail. (By the way, I don't intend to type "Disneyland" for the rest of the story; from now on, it's D-land).

They were passing out party hats at the monorail station. As it so happened, I was going to D-land on the day of its 40th birthday party. Party hats and birthday cake for everyone!

I wandered around D-land for about three hours and had supper, watched a song-and-dance-show, bought souvenirs, and watched a very talented drum and bugle corps. I headed back to the hotel on the monorail and settled into the room for the night.

In the midst of postcard making on my bed, I heard the first booms of the nightly fireworks from D-land. I went to the window and had a perfect view of the whole show, even the grand finale. As a co-worker Chandra would say, Cool! I checked out the schedule for the upcoming meeting and finally said nighty-night to my big empty room.

Day Two, Tuesday

I got up at seven and breakfasted in my room on food I had brought along. The first meeting on my itinerary was the Industry Awards and opening keynote address. The speaker was Eleanor Clift, a well-known reporter from Washington, D.C.. She told stories of life and politics in the nation's capital, and the skeletons in some people's closets. When prompted, she even said a few sentences on healthcare reform. I shuffled on to my first educational lecture, auto-immune diseases, by a well-known researcher from Scripps Research. It was there I soon realized I had forgotten one thing: my stepladder. Without it, everything he said went way over my head (except his sarcastic remarks when they couldn't get the lights turned down to his liking). I hung in there until the break, but decided not to return for part two.

So I wandered outside for fresh air. While standing there and making with my favorite pastime – people watching

– I said to myself, "Self, that woman looks just like Marie." And the response came back, "Self, that's because it *is* Marie."

I immediately hollered at her. She spotted me and came over, where we shared our disbelief at where we all were: Marie, Self and me. Marie and I went to college together and she works at a clinic lab very close to my own, yet we obviously do not communicate often. We took the opportunity to catch up on our gossip and then went our separate ways.

I'd decided at that point I had enough of higher education, so I got on the shuttle bus and went over to the Anaheim Convention Center. This building was huge. The exhibits were in three connected halls, each large enough for a basketball court with bleachers. It was there I stopped for lunch, chicken fajitas and Coke, $9.10. This proved to be the norm for any meal during the week: go ahead and get out a ten-dollar bill.

The exhibits were awesome, putting state exhibits back home to shame. Not to mention the giveaways, cameras, Slinkies, stuffed animals and even free antacids. Now, here is where that little credit card in the registration packet comes in. Say you walk up to a salesman and strike up a conversation about their wonderful product. You chat; he asks if he can send you some information, you say okay. First of all, you would think a company that could afford to send thousands of dollars' worth of instrumentation and booth displays large enough for a ballroom could at least afford to bring along a few lousy pamphlets. But no, they ask for your little credit card with your employer and address and phone number, and they run it through a plain old embosser and add the stamped form to their list of suckers – excuse me – contacts. You know, it's so easy to just hand over that card that by the end of the convention, I could almost make out the writing embossed on it. Then again, maybe I am stretching the truth just a tad.

    I went back to the hotel and checked out the room to see if my roommates Cindy and Leah had arrived. Cindy's luggage was there, and Leah arrived right as I got in. We went down to convention registration and met up with a few others of our Wisconsin delegates. I ended up going back over to the convention center with Sue so she could pick up her DuPont sticker, which I had already done. Armed with these stickers and an invitation, Sue and I were going to the Nixon Library in Loma Linda for a reception, and cocktails and dinner on the Rose Garden lawn.

    After changing into party clothes and taking a series of shuttles and buses from the hotel, we had arrived! There, tuxedoed waiters in white gloves passed out snacks (I can't spell hors-de-overs), manned an open bar and played string quartets while Sue and I took in the historical items of the

Nixon Library. After this, we made our way out to the Rose Garden, followed by the string quartet, of course. They had invited only five hundred guests in total.

Each place setting had a miniature copy of the menu and an engraved, gold-letter opener. Now, you know you have *arrived* when your dinner salad has edible flower blossoms in it and the waiter adds the dressing for you. The rest of the meal was equally high-class, especially the dessert.

After dinner, we got back on the buses for the ride home. Sue was told she could take the centerpiece from our table, and let's just say it was definitely more than three carnations in a plastic vase. After we got on the bus, the man sitting in front of Sue reclined his seat right into Sue's flowers.

Now, I forgot to mention Sue had indulged in a few glasses of wine. She quickly let the guy know just what she thought of his action, and he immediately returned his seat back to an upright position. Then she asked me if she should maybe apologize, which I agreed might not be a bad idea.

Sue proceeded to chat up the guy and his buddy, as all good sales reps do. When we got back to our starting point, I reminded Sue we were still a fifteen-minute shuttle ride from our hotel. She suggested we ask the bus driver for a lift, and lo and behold, the two guys who had been sitting in front of us overheard. They offered us a ride back to our hotel since their business was in California and they were there with their van.

Without much thought, Sue said yes. So these two naïve farm girls from Wisconsin got into a van with two totally strange Californian men. And then ... they drove us back to our hotel, where we cordially thanked them and went straight in. What did you expect? Sue and I are good – probably lucky – girls from Wisconsin, not floozies! I went up to my room and right to bed, but Cindy and Leah didn't get back from D-land until after 1 a.m.

Day Three, Wednesday

We all got up at seven. The logistics of three women getting ready in the same hotel room with only one bathroom is mind-boggling. But we did it, and I headed for more education. I took in back-to-back, hour-and-a-half lectures on OSHA, ergonomics and mailing regulations. I spent part of the afternoon at the exhibit halls. I started with a larger group, but ended up with just the student rep, Brian, sticking around. It amazes me, every time we approached an exhibit booth with an active computer display, he was right there, checking it out. I'm afraid my supervisor, Jan, will have a fit when the result of my freehanded use of my credit card comes to light.

After returning to the hotel, I took the time to explore the hotel grounds. I discovered fishponds, waterfalls you can walk through, gift shops, a wandering group of musicians dressed up like bellboys, and a delicious-looking ice cream shop. A burst of energy hit me, and I went to my room to change clothes. That night, a group of us went over to D-land and immediately lost part of our group. We stayed long enough to take in the fireworks and their great new show, Fantasmic, where they shoot up three fine-spray water displays and project movie segments on them. It was truly fantastic!

And yes, I even got to ride my favorite attraction, It's a Small World. With all that excitement, we got back to our room by midnight. Any more of these long hours, and I was sure my body was bound to rebel.

Day Four, Thursday

Breakfast. Meetings. Lectures. Exhibit hall. D-land.
Been there, done that!

Day Five, Friday

Up again at 7:00, with breakfast on the way to take in another double lecture on mergers. This one cost me $4.25 for an apple, croissant and can of soda. Leah, Cindy and I bummed around the hotel shops for a while in the afternoon. At the beginning of the week, I hinted very strongly that since none of us had anything we had to do for most of Friday, maybe we could make plans to go somewhere else for the day.

I guess I was too subtle; hence, I didn't get to see the ocean. Bummer! Guess I'll just have to go back another time.

During our wandering session around the hotel grounds, we visited that aforementioned ice cream parlor and all splurged on banana splits – at the astronomical price of $4.26! That's $4.26 for one banana split each, not for all three. Gluttony is not cheap in D-land!

We then proceeded on our marathon D-land tour. Boston marathoners have nothing on us. We went from Tomorrowland's monorail station to the restaurant at the Pirates of the Caribbean, vetoed the menu, went to the restaurant at Adventureland, found same opinion of menu there, then hopped back to the monorail station to meet Sue, only to head back to wait in line at the Pocahontas show for an hour, which gave me a well-deserved, albeit standing-up, rest. I figure if horses can do it, there must be some benefit to sleeping standing up.

After the show (technically during the grand finale), we took off for the monorail station again to meet back up with Cindy. We then went to Main Street for a spaghetti dinner at the cafeteria there. We all needed our shoes re-soled after that day. Don't ask me what we saw; I was too busy trying to keep track of my party while not knocking down too many other groups along the way.

By the way, the Pocahontas show was not too bad, on par with the movie, if you get my drift. This, at least, was a live action, singing and dancing show. D-land has a reputation for happy people visiting and happy people working, but I think they forgot that when they designed the stage for this show. The whole thing was slanted, with the backstage higher than the front. This was obviously done to make the show easier to see by the audience, yet the seating was amphitheater style, with each row lower than the one behind. And why did at least half the cast wear ankle or knee braces?

Sue and I (the old folks of the group) went back to the hotel after dinner. I wandered over to the Fantasy Waters show at the back of the grounds, which turned out to be very nice, then back to the room to watch the fireworks for the last time. Got into bed for the night, ahead of Cindy and Leah, who were just back after closing down D-land.

Day Six, Saturday

Last Day In D-Land, There's No Intelligent Life Down Here!

I was up at seven again while the other two slept in; all the while thinking I shouldn't have volunteered for this stupid bylaws seminar for two hours. I'm sorry, I know they did their best to make the meeting interesting, but I mean really, the topic was as exciting as white bread, no mayo. They even had a door prize drawing to spice things up.

I really had hopes for the meeting, which were finally broken when they announced this grand door prize: A copy of "Robert's Rules of Order," Newly Revised. The excitement vibrated through the room, or was that the woman snoring behind me? I did pick up several bits of ammu-information to take back to board meetings.

After the meeting, I went back to the room to get Cindy to straighten out the billing. Remember at the beginning of the week, I put the room on my credit card? Now let's be realistic, do you think I wanted a week's room bill on my card, at $150 a night? Not if I can help it.

I do give the desk clerk credit. It took Cindy and me only three tries to get her to understand what we wanted her to do for us.

Our marathon tour of D-land put me in good practice for the rest of my last day's meetings. I went from the registration desk back to my room to pack (I actually got the suitcase to close) and then on to the meeting room to catch the tail end of the awards ceremonies, staying long enough to hear the closing keynote address. The speaker had a fantastic slide, music and speaking presentation about climbing Mount Everest. I know, it's a far reach to tie in climbing Mount Everest with lab work (then again maybe it's not), but the speaker is married to a medical technologist. The talk was very moving, or was that the memory of my last ride on the monorail?

From there it was back to the room to change into traveling clothes and meet the others to get lunch. We ran to Mazie's Pantry, back to the hotel lobby to eat the sandwiches, and then up to the meeting room for the final business of the convention (at least I think I ate a sandwich; it was all so fast, officer).

Our Wisconsin delegation met outside the meeting room and then waited as two went back for their University of Wisconsin Badgers hats, and another went back for her delegate card. So much for a group photo!

We entered the meeting room together with our red Wisconsin hats on and found we were the only ones decked out in our state colors. It seems that at last year's meeting, many state delegations wore T-shirts or hats from their states, but we were the only ones to uphold this tradition. Oh well, so Wisconsin is cool and with it, and the others are boring.

I was really dismayed when Sue announced she wanted the hats back for next year. Great, now do I not only have the dreaded "hat hair," but I was planning to use the hat on my train trip back home to cover my limp hair. So I had packed my own hat on the bottom of my suitcase and would have to arrive home looking as bad as I had on arriving in D-land. Hey, if you act as if you are supposed to look like a drowned rat, people won't laugh too hard at you. (No charge for the life's philosophy lesson).

The meeting started at 2 p.m. and technically ended at 4 ... until it went 'til 5. I suppose you need this explained.

The items on the agenda are discussed and voted on as needed. There was one slightly exciting topic when we discussed the National Accrediting Agency for Clinical Laboratory Science. The NAACLS rep got up and repeated her performance from the reference committee meeting with an added bonus: She started an inquisition of the American Society for Clinical Laboratory Science president until the chair of the meeting told her enough was enough. (That's not what was said, but I took the time to translate the parliamentary language for you). All that business concluded by 4 p.m., and then started the most ridiculous display of testimonials I have ever sat through.

For an hour we sat while people got up to the microphone and emoted testimonials and thank-yous and gift-givings, the likes of which I hope never to see and hear again. An example: "Jones, speaking for the glorious state of Montana, whereas Susie Squirt has been a fine representative for the entire Region 15, and whereas Susie Squirt has done a wonderful, dedicated job on the education fund committee, and whereas Susie Squirt has done numerous good deeds, and whereas Susie Squirt has succeeded in these endeavors despite her ludicrous name, and whereas I am representing the membership of the wonderful state of Montana as well as the other states in Region 15, Washington, Oregon and Alaska, I would like to declare our heartfelt thanks for her wonderful dedication to the profession and organization of the American Society for Clinical Laboratory Science. We would like her to accept this token of our thanks; it is with great pleasure that I accept this gift in her behalf."

You get the idea? Multiply this hot air by about thirty and we finally got out of that room at 5 p.m.

I still had some time to kill before leaving for the train station, so I made one last foray into the gift shop. I wanted to get a little something for each of my co-workers, my wonderful, beautiful, loving, wonderful co-workers. (Did I lay in on a little too thick? What? You want more? Don't push it, this could get ugly). I was successful in my last shopping trip, and returned to my room for the last time, arranging things just so in my carry-on. It was then time to wait in the lobby for a taxi. Bye-bye, Mickey!

I will always remember – sometimes fondly – the day the elevators all stopped at every floor on the way up and on the way down, the ten-dollar meals, the musical bellboys, the ID badges all with more pins than mine, the miles traveled around D-land even though I actually only saw, at the most, two-thirds of the park. I will be thankful Matt did not share with the rest of the delegation what he and his family had the whole week, the flu. I heard at least five different languages, yet I kept my ears open all week for that Achilles heel of my own, the Southern drawl. I didn't hear it often enough to bring it back home with me, y'all, not like I usually do. Actually, I heard the hard New York accent most of all, and I haven't quite caught the knack of that one yet. Give me time.

The Trip Home, Where No Man Has Gone Before, Exploring Strange New Worlds

Day One, Saturday

I took a taxi to the Amtrak station in Anaheim, a fifteen-minute ride tallied on the taxi's meter by quarters and half-dollars until very quickly it adds up to nearly $10.00. I asked the taxi driver and she (yes, she) told me the stadium which shared its parking lot with the train station was that of the California Angels. I was duly impressed. Yawn.

The train left Anaheim about 6:45 p.m. and I de-trained at Fullerton at 7:30. Rather than go into Los Angeles and back out again to Fullerton, I waited here for the train. Fullerton is not too big. I found a snack bar and got a hot dog and soda a lot cheaper than any meal this past week and ate outdoors, reading until it got too dark. I wandered around a little, too, as much as a fifty-pound suitcase allows you. Part of me regrets I didn't weigh it when I got home, but believe me, it was heavy … and me without my truss!

At 9:30 p.m. we watched the nightly fireworks from D-land. Funny how I still hadn't left it fully behind. The train arrived at 9:50 p.m. and we boarded.

All week I planned two things: That I would take my large suitcase onto the train with me, because the layover in Chicago was too short, and that I would ask, politely, for a window seat.

I did these two things with no problem. It was a wonderful relief! Of course, I sat with a bearded man in his thirties from L.A., but I had a WINDOW SEAT. For those of you who don't understand all the capital letters, I refer you back to earlier in this story.

Anyway, I settled in and fell asleep almost immediately – the best night's sleep I was to have during my adventure.

Day Two, Sunday

I awoke at 5:30 a.m. with a crook in my neck, but otherwise well-rested. I believed at that time my journey was going to cost me several trips to the neck-cracker. And yes, it took about four sessions with the chiropractor to get back to my normal decrepit condition. I washed up as usual, per train-travel accommodations, and checked out the rest of the train, grabbing a Danish and O.J. from the snack bar. The whole operation was virtually the same as the train going south.

I must have been really wiped out from the past week. Even though I took out a book and had my camera ready in my window seat, mostly all I did is sleep. I woke up long enough to notice the book my seat partner was reading, *The Physicists*. It made me wonder what kind of seatmate I had been gifted with, so I struck up an intelligent conversation with him, "That's pretty heavy reading for vacation."

He told me that sort of stuff interested him, that he worked for Ma Bell in L.A. and was on his way to New York for vacation. We conversed inanely for a while. I told him I was on my way home from a medical meeting, and he said he was looking forward to the museums with dinosaurs and stuff in New York. That was it for me; I had plenty of books to read. I wasn't up to any more conversation with a person who read about physics for fun. I picked up my mystery and tuned him out the rest of the trip.

For lunch, I got a sandwich and soda from the snack bar and ate it in the observation car. Eating wasn't too easy. For some reason, I had a very sore mouth, with lots of canker sores on the roof of my mouth. It was particularly bad today, and I ate very slowly. When we got to Albuquerque at about 1 p.m., we were able to get off the train for a short break. I walked over to the station, thinking the restroom facilities would be more spacious than those on the train. Wrong! So I wandered back to the train.

Just in that short time, the heat was unbelievable. I've heard said the heat isn't as bad in the southwest because the humidity is lower, but folks, I've got to tell you ... HOT is HOT! I returned real quickly to the air-conditioned train.

There weren't as many colorful characters this time on the train, but quantity certainly quality made up for quantity I learned this as I went to dinner in the dining car that night. There was a couple sharing the other side of the table with me. Since they never talked to me, I was left to speculate as to their relationship. By my deductions, they were either father/daughter or older husband/younger wife. The other person sitting on my side of the table was a young man with very good table manners and a nice singing voice. I know this not because he talked, but because he played his Walkman with headphones all the time he was sitting at the table, bobbing and singing along with whatever song was playing. Not a favorite student of Miss Manners, I think.

I bet you thought I couldn't run across anyone who could top Typhoid Mary. Wrong. You are so wrong. Let me introduce you to Asthma Alice, who sat right in front of me. Good old Asthma Alice, she was much more interesting than Typhoid Mary. Whereas Mary slept most of the time, Alice slept very little, as she might miss a dose of pills. Alice had bronchitis. Her ritual was fascinating, at least for the first hour or two. It revolved around coughing awhile, mumbling, taking a puff on her inhaler, popping a few and returning to her crocheting. She repeated this cycle every hour or so during the whole trip. Cough, mumble, puff, shake, swallow and crochet. Very distracting, but I didn't mind too much, because I knew I had my most interesting traveler to tell about in my journal.

We traveled through the evening, the sky getting darker as the miles passed. I got tired of sitting and reading, so I stood up and leaned over the seat in front of me. I didn't want to appear rude, so I struck up a conversation with Asthma Alice. Pretty soon we were exchanging crochet patterns. For those of you who disbelieve the domestic side of me, I have swatches of the patterns Alice taught me.

At about 11 p.m., the train slowed down, then halted. The lights went out, the air-conditioning stopped. I saw an engine passing us going in the opposite direction. Small children started crying, everyone started talking. I looked out the window and saw the clearest sky I had ever seen, even picked out the Big Dipper, I think.

An hour passed, and another train passed us in the dark, going the same way. Soon the lights and air-conditioning came back on and we got underway. No official explanation was ever given, which leads to rude awakening No. 2. The rumor Asthma Alice picked up was the week before, an engine had broken down. Now that it was fixed, our train had stopped to pick it up and bring it along. Makes sense, right, even if we are now an hour and a half behind schedule?

After everyone had quieted down from all the excitement, I too, settled in for my last night of sleeping on a train.

Day Three, Monday

I slept poorly and woke at 6 a.m. with another crook in my neck. I wonder if I can get in to the neck cracker tomorrow on my lunch hour. After washing up, I went to the snack bar for breakfast. The orange juice was not a good idea for my sore mouth, and again, there was little conversation with my seatmate. Every time I looked at him, I started wondering, "How do you tell a complete stranger he has a string from his wash cloth stuck in his beard?"

I spent the rest of the day reading, napping, looking out the window and calculating how late we would get into Chicago. It was at least an hour from the time we reached the limits of the Windy City until the train stopped in the station. Not only did it seem the train had to go slowly, but it must pass the station and then reverse its way back in.

My train from Chicago to Milwaukee was scheduled to leave Chicago at 5:04 p.m. As my current one had pulled to a stop in the station at 5:40, I had a problem on my hands. I had a big problem.

Rude awakening No. 3: Amtrak is not sorry if you miss your connection. As a matter of fact, many Amtrak employees don't know the schedules and don't really care to look it up for you if you ask. I attempted to reroute while still on the train, inquiring if there was another train to Milwaukee that night.

The answer I got was, "I don't know, but you can find out in the station."

I made my stumbling way off the train, not in a very great mood, mind you. Remember my description of the "short" walk to the station down the smelly aisles and between the hot trains? You can guess how I felt when I finally reached the information desk.

I asked very politely, through clenched teeth, "Do you have another train to Milwaukee tonight, since you have already made me two hours late? What time will it get to Milwaukee? And will it really get to Milwaukee at 9:37, or will you make me late again? And I won't be able to get my car, because the lot locks at 10:00."

And of course, their answer is so customer-oriented, "Yes, there is a train leaving at 8:50 and arriving at 9:37, and no we cannot guarantee an arrival time … But that train usually runs on time." It made me want to research certain ancient tribes who killed their first born at birth. This helpful clerk would be my candidate for membership.

So I had a couple of hours to kill. Unfortunately, coming in this direction, I could not check my large suitcase, but had to haul it along. This ruled out the second floor food court, as I couldn't find a way up there. I did find a filthy snack shop in the oldest section of the station. I was a little leery, but also hungry. So with one hand on my purse, the luggage between my knees, I sat at a table eating a questionable hamburger (made from an animal which said 'neigh,' not 'moo') and kept one eye on the young gentlemen playing arcade games in the corner. This left me one hand, one eye and a sore mouth to eat with. Ah, fond memories of the Windy City. After I had supped, I returned to the outgoing gate area and waited.

Good news at last! The train left Chicago and arrived in Milwaukee on time. I hauled my suitcase and other luggage onto the train by myself, tearing a fingernail in the process.

I bet you thought I was done with my colorful traveling companions. Hah, never say last. I chatted with my seatmate, probably more than I wanted to because our seat was turned around to face the rest of the them, and the person sitting directly diagonal from me was so interesting I couldn't keep my eyes off her. She was a twenty-ish African-American woman but looked older, perhaps in her thirties, traveling with a two-year-old girl. This woman was fairly big, but her clothes had not caught up with her. She had no upper teeth, and when she ate, it was like watching Grandma with her dentures out. This spectacle was only surpassed by watching her sleep. She also had an infected, pussy eye and definitely was in need of a medical clinic. She was feeding her daughter an egg salad sandwich, occasionally gumming a finger full of filling. After the sandwich, she opened a pudding cup and realized she didn't have any utensils, so she used a corner of the foil lid to spoon out the pudding. Once done, they both fell asleep until we arrived in Milwaukee.

My luck had finally changed, as the train arrived in Milwaukee seven minutes early. I had time to haul my luggage, load it on my wheeled rack and make a dash through the station, across the street, to the still-open parking lot. I slowed to a walk, though, remembering what part of Milwaukee I was in. I loaded my luggage into my trunk and refreshed my memory on how to drive my new car. I pulled out of the lot a little before 10:00 p.m. And yes, I made the wrong turn and had to backtrack my way out of Milwaukee.

The drive home was a blur. I hate driving 65 miles per hour, I hate driving at night and I hate driving long distances. In other words, I finished my vacation with a hateful car ride. But at last I arrived home safely, pulling in to my driveway near midnight. I heaved a sigh of relief mixed with exhaustion, hauling my luggage into the house, greeting my George and generally found everything in fine order. Mom called before I had everything in the house and I assured her I was home and fine. Then I made a beeline for the shower.

I knew in a short while I would have to be getting ready for work, but I had to have that shower. I swear I fell asleep standing there, but managed to turn the water off and get out without falling over. Then it was off to slumberland in my own bed. I know George pestered me to rub his ears as he always does, which I managed in my sleep.

I had hoped for an adventure, and got it in spades!

An Open Door Is Not Always A Good Thing

Introduction

    My stories so far have been Left of Center, and I hope you have enjoyed my sense of humor. This next story is much more Left of Center. It is a true story, a friend witnessed it. It's just that the characters in this story have four legs instead of two! That's right, it's a story of a chipmunk telling a story to his nieces and nephews at a clan gathering. The story involves chipmunks, cats and dogs. So sit back and enjoy, because "this is a true story, you can't make this stuff up."

    My name is Uncle Frank. I hunt with a bunch from the Mason family clan. I also am straddled this evening with one of my two younger brothers, Uncle Floyd, who tends to fall asleep and drool. My other younger brother is Uncle Leo. He is not the brightest peanut in the bird feeder, and he is the subject of this campfire story. Uncle Leo is not here to tell his own version because he is off on another adventure.

The Chipmunk

One day, Uncle Leo decided to go exploring. Known to his younger nephews as Uncle Oh-le, he bravely crossed the wide, dry black river, resting periodically in the tall grass before he moved on. He looked and sniffed as he made his way up the street.

Not far into his excursion, he spotted a yard that looked and smelled intriguing. He made his way up the side of the garage and came to a fence dotted with holes. You know the kind, spaces between the wires big enough for whole families to cross at the same time. So Uncle Leo hopped through, looked up, and smiled.

The yard was a chipmunk's dream come true. There were tall, green needle trees, a whole stretch of beautiful and tasty flowers to tunnel through, a big wooden shed looking quite inviting, a huge old cottonwood tree that was so big around that if Uncle Leo planned to climb it, he would need to pack a bag lunch, and finally the big wooden deck. So inviting.

Uncle Leo decided to explore the deck first. He skipped along the back wall of the garage until he arrived at its base, climbing to the top of the deck using whatever debris he could find to get there. Some of the debris looked interesting and worth exploring; those he filed away for future treks. He edged out onto the deck, picking up sunflower seeds and stuffing them in his cheeks until he thought they would burst. Just when he thought he would have to speak in seeds, he spotted a flower pot and spewed the seeds onto the soil.

That's when he spotted it: the door into the house was open! Granted, it was barely open, but it was enough for a scrawny chipmunk to squeeze through. He started along the deck. He was only a couple of chipmunk lengths away from the opening when he happened to look up into the glass of the door. What he saw was terrifying enough to scare five months off his life.

Reflected in the glass were the figures of two giant dog beasts and their mistress. They were playing some sort of game where the mistress would throw a colorful object across the yard and the two beasts would chase after it. With the beasts distracted, the mistress would bend over and using a metal object, scoop up clumps of dirt and place them in a dark container.

That was all Uncle Leo had time to take in before he gathered his wits about him (all he could find to help him were Dim-Wit, Lazy-Wit, and Quarter-Wit) and squeezed through the opening of the door. He took a look around with all five senses in hyper-drive. Stepping in a little further, his nose was about to get him in trouble.

He smelled something very enticing coming from a bowl only two dog-beast lengths in front of him. He was concentrating on that aroma so much he forgot to engage any other sense. By the time he finally heard the padding of paws and a strange motor-like sound, he knew it was too late.

But the curiosity of wanting to know what was in the room overtook him. He looked up and found himself eyeball to eyeball with the biggest yellow eyes he had ever seen.

He sat up on his back haunches to get a better look, gulping deeply. In a gulp of panic, he started to choke and cough on the sunflower seed that was still lodged in there. When the coughing finally stopped, he peered up again in hopes the sight was only his imagination.

It was not. As a matter of fact, it appeared to be smirking at him.

The Cats

He recognized it from descriptions heard around campfires just like this one. He was facing a big yellow cat. A big yellow cat with a flicking tail, drooling just slightly. He turned away, only to come eyeball to eyeball with another one. This cat was black and white, purring in a definitively feminine voice.

Oh, how his head was swimming. Then he turned his back on the big yellow cat and it was still in front of him.

Poor Uncle Leo, he had all he could to keep from swooning into the black hole that was trying to drag him in. Through the gray mist settling in, he heard all these noises. Noises like mumbling in a strange language, meows of varying attitudes, tails swishing, and lastly, the sound of claws being flexed one by one. *Ping, ping, ping, ping.*

He finally got up his stubborn Dutch pride and decided that if he was about to be devoured, it would not be without a fight. Those two could play all the tricks they wanted, but they would know they had been in a fight. He opened his eyes, raised his head, and looked straight ahead, almost falling into that black hole. He could see there actually were two pairs of cats, each pair was a look-alike for a total of four.

Yet, before Uncle Leo had time to collect his wits, all four began backing away from him, slowly groveling to a new entry into the room. From a doorway down a short hall came the meanest-looking, furriest, growling-est, cat he had never imagined. It came stalking toward him, two heavy paws at a time. She sat on her haunches, curled her tail over her back paws, and spoke.

"Greetings." the new arrival pronounced in perfect Chipmunk. Uncle Leo wondered how this cat had learned

Chipmunk, but thought better of asking under the circumstances. "My name is Kaira, what is yours?"

Uncle Leo responded with another big gulp, trying to muster all his confidence before he answered. "My name is Uncle Leo of the Mason clan."

Kaira broke out into a huge laugh, which sounded more like the sound of a hunting pack. She calmed down and growled something to the other four, making them join in. Finally, they all settled down enough for introductions.

"These two fine strapping males are brothers. Their names are Harley and Davidson. The ladies, and I use the term loosely, are Twilight and her daughter Sweet Pea." Kaira then spoke to the other four cats, each of whom stood up on all four paws and started to mumble.

Then Kaira turned her gaze on Uncle Leo and spoke in Chipmunk again. "It's lunch time, and guess who the main course is!" With this, she took one step toward Uncle Leo. As the black hole reached up to grab him, Uncle Leo vaguely heard a strange commotion from behind.

And then everything went black.

Big, brave Uncle Leo had fainted from fright.

The Dogs

Since Uncle Leo was not able to tell us what happened next, I had to search for an eyewitness to fill in the blanks. It didn't take long. Auntie Fran came to me the next day to tell me all about it. You see, Auntie Fran speaks dog dialect and overheard the big black dog tell the whole story to the neighboring yippy dog.

The cats were ready to pounce on Uncle Leo in one big pack when the two dog beasts and their mistress came back in the very same door Uncle Leo had entered. Those two dog beasts took in the picture very quickly, especially the black one, Baxter. Well, before the mistress could do anything, Baxter charged forward and scattered all the cats, even Kaira. Then he turned, bent over, and sniffed Uncle Leo. The other dog beast, Ginger, was just confused about the commotion between her and her water bowl.

When Uncle Leo didn't move, Baxter touched him with his paw. Now this got Uncle Leo back into action. From here on I go back to Uncle Leo's version, except for the unbelievable parts, because that's Uncle Leo.

The black dog beast slapped Uncle Leo so hard he skidded across the floor, coming to a stop against the glass door he so foolishly breeched a short time ago. The dog beast was having fun as he ran forward, picked up Uncle Leo, turned, and gave his mistress a wink, leaping outside when the mistress opened the door. Baxter ran around the yard, continually tossing Uncle Leo in the air only to run over and start sniffing him with his big black nose.

Soon, Baxter started growing bored and slowed down his tossing game. So when his mistress called him to come in, he only made her wait a short time before leaving his new toy behind. At this point, of course, Uncle Leo was passed out from fright again, and Auntie Fran filled in the next portion of Uncle Leo's harrowing experience.

After a short while, the animal mistress came out with a shovel. That's right, she was going to bury Uncle Leo alive! She dug a shallow grave under the gingko tree, walked over to Uncle Leo, and scooped him up in the shovel. She dumped him in the hole, pushed some dirt over him, and went back into the house.

Very, very fortunately for Uncle Leo, the Mason Clan area is populated by a variety of species that get along with each other. Well, a couple of chickadees were sitting in the gingko tree watching these last sad minutes of Uncle Leo's life. As soon as the mistress turned her back, the chickadees saw a chipmunk tail emerge from the dirt. After some discussion, they flew off and found Uncle Floyd and me.

We followed them back to that horrid yard of torture and found the mound of dirt. We started pulling the dirt aside as fast as we could. Pretty soon, there were four flailing paws helping us. We soon had Uncle Leo sitting on a pile of rose leaves with a dazed look on his face.

And that, my young nieces and nephews, is Uncle Leo's first adventure. He couldn't be here to tell it himself because he is gone on another adventure, which will be number three, if he returns.

Now I will tell you about Uncle Leo's second adventure after a little refreshment! I am simply parched from all that talking and need a few sips of rain water and a sunflower seed or two. Which one of you fine young chipmunks is going to take care of your old Uncle Frank?

And In Conclusion ...

This is not another brilliant short story. This is a thank you from the author, me. I thank you for reading my stories. And an even bigger thank you if you enjoyed them and pass on your positive comments to others. I've enjoyed living through these stories, telling snippets of each experience to any who will listen. But mostly I've enjoyed writing the stories with the encouragement from those to whom I shared the snippets.

Let me just comment about retirement. I've been retired for one year as of this writing, and in that year I have managed to buy a three-wheeled bicycle, fly in a plane for the first time in twenty years, and become an author. Those first two are life-altering for sure. But becoming an author ... that is bucket list material.

As you read in my heart cath story, I generally add things to my bucket lists after the fact. This is the case with becoming an author. I wrote the stories, but I never had a published book in mind when I did the writing. But now, I Am An Author! It is now part of my bucket list and something I consider a way to leave my mark behind.

P.S. I actually own that tie-dye T-shirt used for the cover art!

You can't really be surprised with this embellishment. You just read enough stories written Just Left of Center to expect this.

Acknowledgements

I would like to acknowledge several people who helped me become an author. This is one of my few serious moments, so pay attention please. First, I would like to express my appreciation for the encouragement I received from my many friends and co-workers. This encouragement ran the gamut of loud guffaws while reading to advice to "quit my day job and write full-time."

None of this would have been possible if I had not taken that advice. To be more specific, I did give up my day job by retiring recently. I then took advantage of the Learning in Retirement program offered by the University of Wisconsin-Green Bay Division of Outreach and Adult Access. It is a volunteer program offered with dozens of classes taught by volunteer instructors.

This brings me to the two people who were most helpful in my launch into my second career as an author. Bonnie Groessl and Mike Dauplaise were instructors in one of the first classes I took. Bonnie and Mike own M&B Global Solutions Inc. and helped me publish this book, along with their editing assistant, Amy Mrotek. I am extremely grateful for their guidance throughout this process.

Finally, I would like to thank several of my close friends who appear in these stories. These close friends include Jan, Paula, Lou and Betsy. Hopefully our friendship is strong enough that they won't take offense at my colorful story lines … story lines enhanced by poking friendly fun at these same friends.

Arghhh, I can't stand it any longer. The humorist in me is getting out …

I have a previous experience of making a list of acknowledgements. The large medical clinic from which I recently retired had a practice of honoring its employees. One of the ways was to recognize those employees who had been employed in multiples of five years.

So there I was, at my tenth anniversary recognition. The honorees were asked to say a few words after being announced. So one after the other, said honorees got up and thanked the academy, I mean the clinic, and the doctors and special co-workers. My turn came and the humor devil took hold of my mouth. Out poured a slightly different acknowledgement.

"My name is Fran Gruen. I've been in the lab for ten years, and I have no one I wish to thank. After all, I did it all myself!"

About The Author

I started out as a child. I did start my time on this mad planet growing up in the small village of Kimberly, Wisconsin. In Kimberly, about 90 percent of the households were supported by paychecks from the Kimberly-Clark paper mill. Ours was not one of them.

Kimberly was a predominantly Dutch community, with most grade school classes seated in alphabetical order. Names beginning with "Van" started only halfway through the class. Mine was not one of them. Yet I think these differences served me well in my crazy ride through life.

After graduating in the top fifteen of my high school class, I went on to college at the University of Wisconsin-Stevens Point. I majored and graduated in medical technology. I was a medical technologist for more than forty years. What we do is lab work in hospitals, clinics and research labs. My first professional job was at a small hospital lab for fourteen years, the last eight as the lab manager. Needing a change, I checked around and found my second and final job in Green Bay at a large clinic. It was a wild, fun ride from which I retired earlier this year after twenty-five years.

During my adult life, I have been owned by several different cats. I have my Master Gardener certificate, so I spend most of my time outdoors tending my flower beds.

How did I come to write humorous short stories? My first story, written over twenty years ago, was "How I Spent my Summer Vacation," my story of riding Amtrak for the first time. When I started in Green Bay, I was still active in the local professional group, the American Society for Clinical Laboratory Science. I was on the local board, then the state board, then nominated to attend the national convention in California. I came back from that trip and proceeded to amuse my co-workers, family and friends with stories about this anything-but-boring trip. From there, it was just a small leap into writing down my experiences. A writer was born!

Just Left Of Center

www.ingramcontent.com/pod-product-compliance
Lightning Source LLC
Chambersburg PA
CBHW071520080526
44588CB00011B/1505